Artists
Creating
with Photos

TweetyJill
PUBLICATIONS
makes you creative!

A TweetyJill Publication by Jill Haglund

Featuring well-known artists:

Jill Haglund, Lesley Riley, Claudine Hellmuth, Roben-Marie Smith, Patti Muma,

Kim Henkel, Dawne Renee Pitts, Amy Wellenstein and Helga Strauss

A Note from the Author...

Jill Haglund

Is there *ANYthing* more inspiring than showcasing your photographs in creative, unusual ways? Personally, I don't believe there is. It's just so rewarding to design a "special something" using one of your favorite photos. There is immeasurable value in preserving photos of family, friends and loved ones in your scrapbooks, cards, gifts and displays. It is proof they are dear to your heart!

You are about to have dozens of brand new concepts introduced to you by some of the most innovative artists in the craft industry; I hope you enjoy studying the ideas presented in this book to inspire you to create some of your *own* original treasures with photos, adding of course, your own twist. I know you'll have fun creating these personalized pieces. You're off on an adventure... embrace, explore and enjoy!

It's time to pull out those photographs
and challenge yourself!!

I can't WAIT to get started, how about YOU?

Published and created by TweetyJill Publications
For information about wholesale, please contact customer service at www.tweetyjill.com or 1-941-377-7720
Printed in China • *Artists Creating with Photos* • ISBN 1-891898-07-8
Creative Director, Photo Stylist and Layout: Jill Haglund
Book Design: Laurie Doherty • Editor in Chief: Lisa Codianne Fowler
Phototography: Herb Booth Studio, Inc. • Other Photo Stylists: Lindsay Haglund and Marilyn Haglund

Special Thanks...

I want to thank all of the talented artists involved in the projects in this book. As you will see, the book is all about them and their uniqueness in the world of art as well as crafts. They worked together graciously, allowing "their book" to come together smoothly and with much serendipity! For, although many of them have never met, they worked like a real "team", sending in their one-of-a-kind artwork on a consistent basis and meeting a constant flow of deadlines. And lucky me, it felt like Christmas every week.

Thank you, Ladies!

I feel fortunate to have worked with the caliber of artists whose beautiful treasures inspire us to higher creative levels: Lesley, with her infamous passion for fabrics and photo transfers; Claudine, showing a bright, new colorful palette with her "Poppets"; Roben-Marie with her love of old vintage photographs that inspires us all to dig into our own stash and use them to create something beautiful! Amy's creative clipboards and dimensional gifts are truly ingenious; Patti presents tastefully done composition notebooks that display vintage photos; Dawne and Kim design funky, shabby-chic style pieces that can mesmerize you for hours,

Lisa Codianne Fowler

and Helga inspires us with her tags and cards done in her unique artistic style that everyone so enjoys. Thanks for working so hard, you are a great team! I also want to say an especially gracious thank you to Codi, my Editor In Chief and to Laurie, the designer of Artists Creating with Photos. Laurie's creativity, leadership and determined, dependable effort make this book even more amazing then I envisioned. I appreciate and am in awe of Codi's charming "fresh sparkle" with words, her perseverance through the technical edits and always being there for us with her sunny voice and disposition to match! I admire both of them for their work ethic, ability to focus so intensely and for the special friendship we share.

Laurie Ann Doherty

Table of Contents

CHAPTER 5 Patti Muma

CHAPTER 8 Amy Wellenstein

CHAPTER 9 Helga Strauss

Puppy Love Jill Haglund
Scrapbook Page

"I had just two exposures left in my camera and my daughter, Lindsay, was playing with our dog, Rusty. I got close up and snapped this wonderful, candid shot. When I got my prints back and flipped through them, I was surprised and thrilled by the outcome of this one. It reminded me of a picture of myself when I was little with our cocker spaniel, Taffy. I just knew I had to feature Lindsay's sweet picture in a little journal as a keepsake for her." Jill

Jill Haglund is a mixed media artist, author and instructor. As founder and president of TweetyJill Publications, she has written and published seven books: *Artists Creating with Photos, Creating Vintage Cards, Vintage Collage for Scrapbooking, The Idea Book for Scrapbooking, Scrapbooking for Kids (ages 1-100), Scrapbooking as a Learning Tool* and *The Complete Guide to Scrapbooking.*

Jill has instructed at national conventions, tradeshows, retail camera shops, and specialty rubberstamp and scrapbook stores. She has organized weeklong workshops at The International Scrapbook Convention, Cord Camera and Miles Kimball's Exposures retail store. Many of her collaged scrapbook pieces are on display in shadowboxes at the Exposures Gallery outside New York. She has been involved with craft store grand openings and taught weekend classes at Barnes & Noble Booksellers.

Currently she is excited about her new opportunity to teach summer workshops in Tuscany, Italy, which combine countryside tours and village shopping trips for ephemera with art techniques, rubberstamping and collage. The workshop concludes with a lively gathering during a sumptuous, regional dinner that everyone participates in preparing.

Jill says, "I love ANYTHING that has to do with art, photos, paper and/or rubber stamps! Rubberstamping, making cards and keeping arty journals has been my obsession of late! It is so therapeutic and relaxing to express yourself in any art form. I want everyone to be able to have the ability to enjoy it as much as I do. That is what motivates me to do craft books and teach classes.

I love to bring out the creativity within people when I am in a class setting; facilitate just enough to allow them to explore and discover what they already have inside. Everyone seems to say 'I am not creative' or 'I am not artistic.' I feel everyone has potential far beyond what they believe. What I delight in the most is encouraging others; getting people excited about their capabilities, taking the fear out of artistic expression and making it a positive experience! I want people to enjoy their time creating and to develop a passion for seeking ideas and learning new things and to leave with a new sense of freedom. I truly believe discovering, exploring and creating can be so much fun! "

Materials:

Scrapbook: DMD Industries
Dictionary Thoughts Paper: Real Life by Pebbles, Inc.
Postage Paper, Large Number Cream/Red: Mustard Moon
Adhesive-Backed Words/Letters: Pebbles, Inc
Bubble Type Letters: Li'l Davis Designs
Tags (coffee-dyed): Local Craft Store
Wooden Clip: 7gypsies
Bulldog Clip: Local Office Supply
Round Metal Discs: Li'l Davis Designs

Adhesives: Xyron Machine; The Ultimate! Glue
Other: Strong coffee (for painting inside edge of scrapbook pages)
Tools: Sandpaper and stapler

Instructions:

Paint inside scrapbook pages with strong coffee. Roll "dictionary thoughts" paper through Xyron and apply to page; trim. Glue on small and large coffee-dyed tags. Lightly sand (to give an aged appearance) and staple number "2" onto large tag. Clip on tag with bulldog clip. Apply all stickers. Place bubble letters into metal discs and glue onto small tags with The Ultimate! Glue, then glue to journal page. Slip on wooden clips.

Vintage Travel Log Jill Haglund

I love photos of old vintage cars. Back in those days everyone was so proud of their cars, and they liked to have their pictures taken with them. You can always see the pride on their faces. This particular old car happens to have been owned by my husband's side of the family, the Larsons. If you look at the photo through a magnifying glass, you can see the date on it is 1919 and that it was taken outside the Chevrolet dealer in Isle, Minnesota. The car has paper ribbons wrapped around the wheels. It looks like this lucky man just struck a deal on a brand spanking new Chevrolet.   Jill

Materials:

Scrapbook: DMD Industries

Holiday Stripe Paper: K&Company

Barnyard Willow Paper: Real Life by Pebbles, Inc.

Measurement Paper: 7gypsies

ABC's Stickers, Sampler Travel Stickers, Travel Definitions, Word Strips Stickers and Label Stickers: Real Life by Pebbles, Inc.

"Traditions" Bubble Word: Li'l Davis Designs

Collage and Stitched Tags: Real Life by Pebbles, Inc

Black StazOn Solvent Inkpad: Tsukineko

Acrylic Golden Ochre Acrylic Paint: Delta

Torn Notebook Border Rubber Stamp: Stampotique Originals

Vintage Man Rubber Stamp: River City Rubber Works

Small Alligator Clip, Metal Definition ("Destination"), Watch Charms, Small Key and Small Lock: K&Company

Green Eyelets: Making Memories

Keys: Li'l Davis Designs and Stampington & Company

Metal Disk for Bubble Word: Li'l Davis Designs

Adhesives: Yes! Paste; The Ultimate! Glue

Other: Photograph and twine

Tools: Eyelet setter, hammer and medium-sized artist's paint-brush and bulldog clips

Instructions:

TRAVEL LOG COVER: Adhere K&Company paper to cover front of scrapbook; trim to fit. Attach metal definition and sticker letters. Collage tags with stickers, letters, words and metal pieces. Attach tags, key and watch faces to side spiral binding.

PAGE ONE: Paint the first blank page and one inch inside of second blank page with a wash of Golden Ochre paint. Stamp vintage man and torn notebook border in black. Glue Measurement paper. Cut two squares of paper, add eyelets and thread with twine. Trim as desired; tie and glue to outer corners. Hold with bulldog clips until dry. Adhere "tradition" into disc and glue in place. Position two keys and small lock.

PAGE TWO: Cover page with green paper; trim and adhere photo. Punch through twill, set eylets. Add all definitions and sticker letters. Attach small alligator clip.

Artist's Photo Blocks

Jill Haglund

Materials:

Papers: K&Company and 7gypsies

Vintage Postcards: Vintage Charmings

Adhesive-Backed Words/Letters: K&Company and Pebbles, Inc.

Definitions: FoofaLa

Transparencies: K&Company

Lumiere Acrylic Paints: Jaquard Products

Craft Inkpads: Colorbox by Clearsnap

Black StazOn Solvent Inkpad: Tsukineko

Children's Faces Rubber Stamps: Paperbag Studios

Four to Six 2" Wooden Blocks: Local Craft Store

Pewter Frame: Making Memories

Adhesives: Xyron Machine or Yes! Paste; E-6000

Other: Photos, papers and vintage buttons

Tools: Marvy Uchida Embossing Heat Tool and craft knife

Instructions:

1. Paint blocks with Lumiere paints. Let dry or use heat tool to reduce drying time.

2. Apply all rubberstamp images. When rubberstamping images, use Craft ink and dry completely with heat embossing tool.

3. Cut and apply lighter weight items (papers, definitions, transparencies, ephemera and postcards) using a Xyron machine or Yes! Paste. Dry overnight if using paste. Once dry, trim all paper edges with a craft knife.

4. Add pewter frame, buttons and bulkier items with E-6000 adhesive. Dry overnight.

Use these instructions as a guide. Decorate your blocks with personal sayings, rubberstamp images and meaningful photos as inspired.

Ideas: *Personalized birthday gift, wedding or graduation gift with names, date and photos (use gold or silver trim on all edges of blocks), teacher gift, personalized shower gift or new baby gift with name and birth information along with photos, postcards or other paper images of babies. This is a great craft to do with a group of teenage girls.*

I first made these as a gift for my teenage daughter. She loved the personal little wooden "pieces of art", with special messages just for her. Since, I have made several personalized sets for relatives, girlfriends or special occasions. They are always a big hit because of their uniqueness.

Jill

My Wonderful Button Box Jill Haglund

My grandmother had a large tin full of buttons that I loved as a little girl. I remember playing in it for what seemed like hours, looking at all the beautiful designs and recognizing my grandma's winter coat button or the ones on her spring dresses. Maybe I loved the buttons because they reminded me of her, and I dearly loved my grandmother. What I would give to have that button box. So, I decided to make my own! " Jill

Materials:

Gold Crafters Inkpad: Colorbox by Clearsnap

Burgundy and Gold Acrylic Paints: Delta

Green Patina Paint: Local Craft Store

Crackle Paint Medium: Anita's Fragile Crackle

Starburst Rubber Stamp: Rubber Stampede

Gold Skeleton Leaf: Black Ink

Large Flat Glass Bead and Letter Beads: Local Craft Store

Drawer Handle: Local Hardware Store

Pewter Frame: Making Memories

Key and Keyhole: Li'l Davis Designs

Brass Corner: Fancifuls, Inc.

Adhesives: E-6000; Non-Yellowing, Acid-Free Mod Podge by Plaid

Other: Photographs, cigar box, Domino game piece, Scrabble wood tiles, paper ephemera, postage stamps and vintage buttons

Tools: Marvy Uchida Embossing Heat Tool and regular 1" paintbrush (do not use foam brush)

Instructions:

1. Paint box gold and let dry.
2. Apply crackle medium and let dry.
3. Paint over crackle medium with desired color.
4. Wait overnight until it "crackles" and completly dries.
5. If applying patina to brass corner, simply rub it into the creases, wipe off slightly and let dry prior to adhering to corner of box..
6. Apply photos under large glass piece and frame.
7. Gather the collection of materials for decorating your box and adhere light weight items by brushing them with Mod Podge by Plaid.
8. Adhere heavier items with E-6000.

This is a real hodgepodge of collage items that make me smile. *I love vintage photos, art emphemera, anything related to the city of Paris, Scrabble tiles and metal pieces for added texture. On "My Wonderful Button Box" I incorporated all of them and added a drawer handle to open it. Inside are hundreds of genuine vintage buttons I have collected while scouring anitque shops, flea markets, garage sales and thrift stores. Some of my most* favorite *buttons are passed along to me from friends who know I love them!* Jill

Bride Getting Ready Jill Haglund
Wedding Card

Materials:

Large, Pre-folded Ivory or White Cards: Local Craft Store

Original Old Photo Postcard and Script Papers: Vintage Charmings

Marbled Paper: Paper Passions

Hand-Dyed Silk Ribbon (1/2"): JKM Ribbons and Trims

Heart Charm: Fancifuls, Inc. or Local Craft Store

Adhesives: Yes! Paste; Sobo Craft and Fabric Glue

Other: Lace, sheet music and canceled postage stamps

Instructions:

Color copy postcard and cut out image as desired. Paste script paper smoothly to front of pre-folded card as the background. Collage torn sheet music and postage. Paste marbled paper to bottom as border. Paste down postcard image. Press and dry flat. Once dry, add lace trim with Sobo Glue. Press and dry again. Tie with ribbon and add charm.

Vintage Couple Jill Haglund
Anniversary Card

Materials:

Large, Pre-folded Ivory or White Cards: Local Craft Store

Original Old Photo Postcard and Postcard Front with Postage: Vintage Charmings

Marbled Paper: Angy's Dreams

Hand-Dyed Silk Ribbon (1/2"): JKM Ribbons and Trims

Heart Charm: Fancifuls, Inc. or Local Craft Store

Adhesives: Yes! Paste; Sobo Craft & Fabric Glue

Other: Lace with beads and sheet music

Instructions:

Color copy postcard and cut out image as desired. Paste marbled paper smoothly to front of pre-folded card as the background. Collage old postcard pieces, torn sheet music and postcard image. Press and dry. Add lace trim to top and bottom and top as borders with Sobo Glue. Press and dry again. What a great way to recycle! They are creative, quick and fun to make. It's a rewarding way to fill your creative yearning with the least amount of mess. Small canvas - small cleanup.

Every time I see beautiful vintage postcards I think of creating soft, elegant collaged cards around a theme... wedding, anniversary, baby arrival, fathers day. Somehow each postcard seems to speak to me about how to turn it into something useful again. Jill

Friends Jill Haglund

Bright & Colorful Acrylic Frame

Materials:

Colorful Cardstock, Pack of Colored Tissue Paper: Local Craft Store

Phrase Café Sticko Stickers: EK Success

Bulldog Clips: Local Craft Store

Adhesives: Xyron Machine or PVA; The Ultimate! Glue

Other: Photograph, two acrylic pieces for frame - one 7 1/2" x 9 1/2" and a smaller one, 4"x 6" for placing over picture, buttons, ribbons, small 3/4" bolts and nuts with washers, 3 1/2" screw and bolt for stand

Tools: Drill and drill bit for size of bolts you have chosen and permanent pen to mark acrylic

Jessica

Floral Acrylic Frame

Jill Haglund

Materials:

Pink Cardstock, White Lace Rice Paper:
Local Craft Store

Floral and Butterfly Tissue Paper and Gold Text Tissue Paper:
Local Craft Store

Phrase Café Sticko Stickers:
EK Success

Brass Corner, Leaf and Butterfly: Local Craft Store

Gold Skeleton Leaf: Black Ink

Magenta and White Toule, Fabric with Gold Stars, Ribbon and Mesh: Local Craft or Fabric Store

Bulldog Clips: Local Craft Store

Adhesives: Xyron Machine or PVA Glue; The Ultimate! Glue and E-6000

Other: Photograph, two acrylic pieces for frame - one, 7 1/2" x 9 1/2" and a smaller one, 4"x 6" for placing over photo, small glass pebble, lace, postage, small 3/4" bolts and nuts with washers, 3 1/2" screw and bolt for stand

Tools: Drill and drill bit for size of bolts you have chosen and permanent pen to mark acrylic

Instructions (same on both frames):

1. Measure, mark and drill holes in the frame as indicated in the photo.

   Drilling instructions below:

   SIDE RIBBON EMBELLISHMENT: Measure, mark and drill holes 1" apart on left side of frame. (on "Friends" only)

   PHOTO PROTECTOR: Place smaller piece of acrylic over the larger piece (frame) in the area you want your photo to be positioned; mark top and bottom center, drill.

   STAND: Drill hole in center 3/4" up from bottom.

2. Select papers you think express a mood you want to convey or that tie in with the theme of your photo. This frame was done completely in tissue papers. Tissue is lightweight, pliable and easy to fold over the acrylic without tearing the corners.

3. Tissue papers are too thin to run through the Xyron machine without backing them first. Run an 8"x10" sheet of copy paper through the Xyron machine, peel off back and apply cut pieces of colorful tissue paper onto your paper, covering entirely.

4. Run the side without tissue paper back through the Xyron machine again. Peel and slowly press onto the front of your acrylic frame. Fold over back and adhere (miter-fold the corners).

5. Use an awl to poke a small hole from the back, through the drilled holes, to the decorative side (to help you see where to attach picture later).

6. For back: Place frame on piece of colorful cardstock and trace; cut paper slightly smaller then traced line (1/8" all the way around). Send cut paper through the Xyron machine. Peel, hold down curl and run a thin strip of The Ultimate! Glue around the inside sticky edge of paper, adhere to back of frame and hold with bulldog clips. Wipe off any excess glue. Dry overnight.

7. In the back of frame, using the awl, again poke small holes through previous drilled holes and pokes to indicate where to place your bolts.

8. Place picture behind smaller acrylic piece and use small bolts, washers and nuts to hold it to frame. Tighten firmly. Add 3" bolt for frame stand.

9. If applicable (on"Friends" only): Thread and double-tie colorful ribbons to the side of the frame; add buttons with The Ultimate! Glue.

10. Press on word stickers.

Instructions Page 20

Spring Journal Lesley Riley

"*This is one of my favorite photos of my granddaughters. The forsythia in the background lets you know it's spring! I chose the bright green and floral fabrics to make a page that looks as fresh as spring itself.*" Lesley

Lesley Riley is best known for her "Fragment" series of small fabric collages. She is also a nationally-known collage artist, art quilter and dollmaker with a passion for color and the written word. Leslie teaches an array of mixed-media workshops from coast to coast. Her art and articles have appeared in numerous books and magazines and she is awaiting publication of her first book. Lesley is also Arts Editor of the new mixed media magazine, *Cloth Paper Scissors*. Through her art, writing and teaching, Lesley aspires to inspire others to find their own voice and create their art.

Lesley writes: "My art is about the magic of making art ... the how, the why, the what, even the where has unending fascination for me. My work reflects my life. My family is always present in my art. In the irregularity of my stitches when my ten year old runs up next to me to show me her latest creations. In the spontaneity of a stolen moment to adjust a composition. In the unexpected color combinations I find after the girls have had a go at my fabric stash.

Art is a way of life in our house. I can teach my children now what it took me over 40 years to discover ... that creating, making art, is a natural, free-flowing process that requires no special time, no secluded space, no Masters of Fine Art."

Naturally, you want to see my art. My creations. My soul made visible. Everyone is curious to see what others have created to see if they can find any meaning in it for themselves. Leo Tolstoy said, "Art is a microscope which the artist fixes on the secrets of his soul and shows to other people these secrets which are common to all." Lesley

Materials:

Journal: 7gypsies

Printed Twill Tape: 7gypsies

Fabric: Learning Cursive by 3 Sisters

Mittens: Wimpole Street Creations

Stars: Dennison

Adhesives: Sobo Craft & Fabric Glue

Other: Wooden Scrabble tiles and Fabric

Instructions:

1. Glue 3 Sisters' fabric to page.

2. Glue other fabric scraps and lace to page.

3. Scan and print photo and quote onto fabric.

4. Glue photo onto page, then mittens and twill tape.

5. Adhere stars in random pattern.

6. Spell "Winter Wonderland" with wooden Scrabble tiles and glue to page.

"I bought these mittens years ago after seeing a framed collection of old ones. There's something so innocent about mittens. When I came across them in my stash, I knew that I wanted to create a page around them."

Lesley

Winter Wonderland Journal
Lesley Riley

Spring Journal pg 18

Materials:

Tall Book Journal: 7gypsies

Definitions, Foofa-Lopes Rectangle and Shabby Labels: FoofaLa

Aged Typewriter Letters: Nostalgiques by Rebecca Sower/EK Success

Index Tabs: 7gypsies

"Heart in Bronze" Metal Tag Blanks: FoofaLa

White Paint Pad Pigment Inkpad: Rubber Stampede

Stylus: Local Craft Store

Decorative Nail Heads (#11520G Filigree Gold): Jewel Craft

Eyelets: Local Fabric Store

Inkjet-Ready Fabric: Color Textiles, Inc.

Wonder Under Fusible Interfacing: Pellon

Adhesives: Sobo Craft & Fabric Glue

Other: Fabric

Tools: Home-Pro LR by American Tag

Instructions:

1. Scan and print photo and quote on inkjet-ready fabric; iron Wonder Under to back of fabric.

2. Cut out photos and quote.

3. Create collage with fabric scraps; iron photos and quote to fabric collage to adhere.

4. Set decorative nail heads into fabric with Home-Pro tool.

5. Cut Shabby Label in half and tone down color with white inkpad. Arrange behind fabric and glue label and fabric layers together.

6. Spread thin, even layer of Sobo Craft & Fabric Glue to page and glue completed fabric collage to pages.

7. Cut definition of spring from card and glue inside envelope; glue envelope to page.

8. With stylus or other metal tip, write names on heart tag and glue to page.

9. Add typewriter letters to tabs and attach to journal pages with eyelets.

Materials:

Journal: Naked Gypsy by 7gypsies

Ribbon: Morex Corporation

Heart Button: JHB International

Color #712 Embroidery Floss: DMC

Inkjet Ready Fabric: Printed Treasures by Millikan

Wonder Under Fusible Interfacing: Pellon

Safety Pins: Making Memories

Adhesives: Sobo Craft & Fabric Glue

Other: Additional fabric

Instructions: Scan and print photos and quote on fabric; iron Wonder Under to back of fabric. Cut out photos and quote. Create collage with fabric scraps; iron photos and quote to fabric collage to adhere. Pin through all layers with safety pins. Sew or glue button to center collage using 6 strands of embroidery floss. Spread thin even layer of Sobo Craft & Fabric Glue to page and adhere completed collages.

Shared Joy Cover Instructions:

Glue frayed edged fabric to the covers of the journal. Tie ribboon around each side of the two-sided journal cover, making the bows meet in the middle/front of the cover.

Shared Joy Lesley Riley
Journal

To show a child what once delighted you, to find the child's delight added to your own, this is happiness.
J. B. Priestley

"I came across this quote about the same time I found the photo of the little girl painting. The triple spread inspired me to search through my photo collection to find other pictures of things that I hope to pass on to my children … the things that bring me *joy*." Lesley

*"On one of my many visits to the craft store I spied this bicycle sticker and instantly knew that I had to do a page juxtaposing the sticker with my photo of a girl and her bike. I used to spend hours riding my bike. It's one of a **child's first freedoms**, to explore the neighborhood on her very own bike."* Lesley

My Bike Journal Lesley Riley

Materials:

Journal: Naked Gypsy by 7gypsies

Stickers: PSX (Personal Stamp Exchange)

Definitions Seasons Pack: FoofaLa

Alphabet Tiles: PaperBliss by Westrim

Dark Moss Ink: Colorbox Fluid Chalk Inkpads by Clearsnap

Wonder Under Fusible Interfacing: Pellon

Pearl Nickel 3/16" Seeded Nail Head: Lost Art Treasures

Adhesives: Sobo Craft & Fabric Glue; Gem-Tac Permanent Adhesive by Beacon

Other: Fabric

Tools: Home-Pro LR by American Tag

Instructions: Scan and print photo on fabric; iron Wonder Under to back of fabric. Cut out photo.

Create collage with fabric scraps, then iron photo to fabric collage to adhere. Adhere PSX bicycle sticker to fabric. Attach nail heads to photo corners and bike wheels hubs using American Tag Setting Tool.

Cut definition from sheet. Edge with inkpad to define edge. Glue definition to collage with Sobo Craft & Fabric Glue. Glue Alphabet Tiles to fabric using Gem-Tac glue.

Spread thin even layer of Sobo Craft & Fabric Glue on page and adhere completed collage.

Fragments
by Lesley Riley

My "Fragment" series came about as a result of having lots of ideas and little time. I started creating small fiber collages one frozen January day when the power was out. Each one inspired another until I had a stack of more than 25. They came fast and easy.
The daylight faded away but the creative fire never did. I have been creating "Fragments" for over five years, and I am still amazed by the beauty of each one and the joy it brings me.

Fragment (frag'ment), n., v. - n. Figurative: a part of an incomplete or unfinished work, also a surviving part of something lost or no longer in existence.

The real mirror of your life and soul is your true friend. A friend helps you glimpse who you really are and what you are doing here.   John O'Donohue

"I love fabric. I love playing around and juxtaposing one piece with another, tossing a piece on the table and having it fall next to another, presenting a new, unthought-of, combination that excites the eye. Unthreading the fabric to discover the beauty of it's weave I also find my way through my spiritual and artistic journey. Think of my fragments as your game piece. Now you make the next move. Frame it; make it part of a quilt… a purse, pillow or personal talisman. Take it. Make it yours." Lesley

Five Tag Book Lesley Riley

Materials:

Tag Book (#8): 7gypsies

Black Paper: Local Craft Store

Adhesive-Backed Words/Letters: Life's Journey Domed Random Alphabet; Clearly Yours by K&Company

Tea-Stained ABC and Number Tags: Nostalgiques by Rebecca Sower/EK Success

True Poppy Paint: Aleene's Premium Coat Acrylic

Yellow Cadmium Inkpad: ColorBox Fluid Chalk Inkpads by Clearsnap

"Measure Up" Ribbon: Offray

Clothespins: 7gypsies

Adhesives: Sobo Craft & Fabric Glue; GE Silicone II Household Glue

Other: Twine, aluminum number "5"

Tools: ColorBox Foam Stylus

Instructions:

Color journal page with ColorBox Fluid Chalk Inkpad, using direct-to-paper method, (rubbing ink directly onto page with inkpad or a ColorBox Stylus).

Glue ribbon along bottom of page. Paint aluminum number and clothespins with Aleene's True Poppy; let dry. Scan and print photos onto fabric or paper. Back number and one photo with black paper. Tie twine in adhesive-backed number tags and adhere tags to ribbon. Glue black paper-backed photo and number to page. Glue fabric photo to page. Print quote onto vellum and glue to page. Attach painted clothespins to top of page as if holding photo on. Adhere letters to photo to spell "five."

"I just love this quote. Imagine still being friends with someone you knew when you were *five*. It is rare in this day and age. I found this little photo in my collection. I *pretend* it's me and five friends. The tape measure ribbon reinforced the number theme and the red adds the punch that brings the page alive." Lesley

Materials:

Tag Book (#8) and Papers: 7gypsies

"Memories" Bubble Phrase:
L'il Davis Designs

Yellow Cadmium Dye Ink: ColorBox
Fluid Chalk Inkpads by Clearsnap

Ribbon: Lingerie Ruban by 7gypsies

Adhesives: Sobo Craft & Fabric Glue

Other: Vintage velvet flower

Instructions:

1. Add Colorbox ink to paper using direct-to-paper method; glue paper to page.
2. Fold a length of ribbon in half and glue ribbon to page.
3. Scan and print photo onto fabric or paper; glue photo over ribbon and onto page.
4. Glue vintage flower over photo.
5. Attach adhesive Bubble Phrase to ribbon leaf.

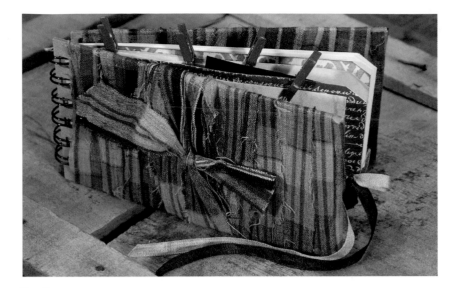

This tiny tag book is the perfect place for photographic memories. I wanted to set the stage with the opening page, with just a few elements that would carry the tone for the pages to come. I envision the ribbon threading through all of the tags, tying all my memories together. **Lesley**

Memories Tag Book Lesley Riley

Coney Island Journal
Lesley Riley

"Chancing upon a collection of photobooth photos, I couldn't resist creating my own fabric photobooth montage. That spiral binding was just begging for a little embellishment and I pulled out my hand-dyed ribbon to tie a few jaunty bows. Before I knew it, there was one on every spiral." Lesley

Materials:

Tall Book Journal: 7gypsies

Aged Typewriter Letters: Nostalgiques by Rebecca Sower/EK Success

Ivory Mini Scallop Tag: Creative Tags

Index Tabs: 7gypsies

Yellow Cadmium Inkpad: ColorBox Fluid Chalk Inkpads by Clearsnap

White Gelly Roll Pen: Sakura

Metallic Green Soliheads (Nail Heads): Coffee Break Design (available through Marco Paper)

Eyelets: Local Craft Store

Inkjet-Ready Fabric: ColorTextiles

Wonder Under Fusible Interfacing: Pellon

Adhesives: Sobo Craft & Fabric Glue

Other: Fabric and ribbon

Tools: Japanese screw punch, embroidery needle

Instructions:

1. Scan and print photos on inkjet-ready fabric. Iron Wonder Under to back of fabric.

2. Cut out photos.

3. Create collage with fabric scraps. Iron photos to fabric collage to adhere.

4. Punch holes into fabric layers with Japanese screw punch and set rivets into fabric.

5. Write names on tags. Add color to tags and edges with Yellow Cadmium ink.

6. Thread 1/8" ribbon and sew tags onto fabric.

7. Spread thin even layer of Sobo Craft & Fabric Glue on page and glue completed fabric collage to pages. Add text with white Gelly Roll pen.

8. Cut ribbon to approximately 6" lengths and tie around spiral binding.

9. Add typewriter letters to tabs and attach to journal pages with eyelets.

"There's magic in art. Making art makes us happy. Creating fulfills the eternal longing of the soul. Our soul craves expression. Art is the soul made visible. I create and show my art so that others can get to know the real me. Through my art I hope to inspire others and share the magic." Lesley

On the Range Box Claudine Hellmuth

*When I created this piece I was teaching a workshop in
Sedona, Arizona, home to cowboys and cowboy lore. I left
in a "western" mood and decided to create a piece to
represent this special place.* Claudine

Instructions Page 31

Claudine Hellmuth is a mixed-media collage artist from Orlando, Florida, who has been working in collage for about eight years. She went to school in Washington, DC and graduated with a Bachelor's Degree in Fine Arts in 1997. Claudine conducts workshops throughout the United States and enjoys teaching and meeting students who also like to create with collage. Her techniques are described in her book, *Collage Discovery Workshop.* She also creates artwork for illustration and for the licensing markets; her designs are on greeting cards, journals, posters, magnets, blankets and more.

Claudine wrote: "My work has undergone a drastic change in the last year. It went from the romantic, nostalgic style I had been working in for close to six and a half years to the more whimsical work I am creating now. What signaled the change was a desire to try something new. I had become very comfortable with my artistic patterns and, as a result, instead of being excited about my work, it felt more like I was simply going through the motions … repeating ideas and compositions I had done in the past.

I had just finished writing my book, Collage Discovery Workshop, and I felt burned out. I felt my work needed a change and it took me almost a year and a half of experimenting to arrive at my new look. I played around with images and ideas, and made lists of the types of artwork I enjoyed looking at.

After making many lists, I looked at what I had written. My list of things I liked consisted of texture, line, whimsical themes, bright colors and drawing. Most of all I wanted to bring more drawing back into my work and create with collage by using more of my own images. At first, I felt that I needed to draw realistically, almost as if to prove that I could. Yet when I looked at the works of artists who drew in a stylized and whimsical manner, I discovered that I enjoyed them more than if they had been drawn realistically. Why then, did I feel the need to prove something with my drawing ability when I liked whimsical drawing by other artists?

I decided it was my ego getting in the way and that I would explore whimsical drawing and bring that into my collage, along with the other items from my research. It was a period of much growth and change. Along with drawing, color and texture, I also wanted to bring more enjoyment into my work.

Now I'm having fun and making myself giggle and laugh while I work and play with my new images and characters. It's a good feeling. I wanted to give these new works a name to separate them from my other collage style. After much thought, I decided to call them 'Poppets.' My grandma used to use the word "poppet" as a term of endearment, often saying to me, 'Don't worry little poppet everything is going to be OK.' And since these new works make me feel good, safe and young, the name fit perfectly.

I see myself doing collage for many years ahead, because it has many possibilities and offers so many different ways of working. Collage can be layered or minimal, serious or funny. I don't think I'll run out of ways of incorporating it into my artwork. For now, I'd like to continue working on my new Poppet series … and see where it takes me."

A Little Birdie Told Her - Tag Book

Claudine Hellmuth

> " I love using text as a starting point for collage ideas. I found the text "a little birdie told her" and it sparked the theme for this tag book. "
>
> Claudine

Materials:

Marble Paper: Angy's Dreams

Tag Book: 7gypsies

Pyrrole Red and Titanium White Acrylic Paint: Golden Artist Colors

Black Marker in .3 nib (to draw black lines): Coptic

Image of Girl's Face: ARTchix Studio

Waxed Thread: 7gypsies

Adhesive: Regular Gel Matte by Golden

Tools: Star Punch by Marvy

Instructions:

Cover: Lightly draw tree and bird with pencil. Paint both with acrylic paint. Paint a red house with dotted lines. Draw fine lines with marker to finish drawing.

Inside: Punch stars out of blue paper and glue to tag. Cut out and glue down photo image for a head and green paper for a skirt. Add drawn lines to finish body. Add red dotted lines to make a house shape. Add text to complete the piece and journal as desired.

On the Range Box pg 28

Materials:

Papers: Making Memories

Collage Head of Boy: Lost Aussie Designs

Shadow Box: Crafters Edition

Hansa Yellow Medium and Cobalt Teal Acrylic Paints: Golden Artist Colors

Markers: Permapaque by Sakura

Adhesive: Regular Gel Matte by Golden

Instructions:

Paint the box to your liking; create green grassy hills using acrylic paint in the background to add depth. Cut out head from Lost Aussie Designs or use your own photo. Create body using paper by cutting out pants, shirt, books and boots. Outline with pen to add detail. Cut out dog shape; add marker detail again. Glue items in the box as desired. If you would like your images to have more dimension, consider adding foam dots to the back of your pieces so they are raised up from the background.

"I got the idea for this book when I was at the children's section at the book store. I saw a few flip books and I thought it would be fun to do the same with my *Poppet designs*." Claudine

Mix & Match Flip Book
Claudine Hellmuth

Materials:

Assorted Scrapbook Papers: Local Craft Store

The "Maison" Journal: 7gypsies

Titanium White, Titan Buff, Cobalt Teal and Pyrrole Red Acrylic Paints: Golden Artist Colors

Black Marker in .3 nib (to draw black lines): Coptic

Adhesive: Regular Gel Matte by Golden

Other: Newspaper

Tools: Loew Cornell Spongits 508 Multipack (to sponge on dots on inside cover with white paint) and Jacquard squeeze bottle with .5mm nib (used with red acrylic to draw in red dotted line around house)

Instructions:

Paint house-shaped journal cover to your liking. Cut inside pages into three horizontal sections with scissors. Copy four heads on a copying machine. Paste into the top most section on each page. Complete heads, torsos and feet for each section and color. Use colored papers as desired for clothes.Use newspapers for clothes and paint over them with Titan Buff acrylic paint. Create a "mix and match" flip book; it's your chance to enjoy being a kid again!

Purple Shopping Girl Card
Claudine Hellmuth

Materials:

Watercolor Paper or Pre-Folded Watercolor Cards:
Canson

Various Printed Papers, Tissue Papers or Fabrics:
Local Craft Store

Titan Buff, Cobalt Teal and Pyrrole Orange Acrylic Paint: Golden Artist Colors

Purple Marker: Permapaque by Sakura

Head Images: Lost Aussie Designs

Black Marker in .3 nib (to draw in black lines): Coptic

Adhesive: Regular Gel Matte by Golden

Other: Newspaper

Tools: Circle Punch by Marvy Uchia and Paper Shapers by Provo Craft

Instructions:

Cut watercolor paper to size and fold in half for card or buy Canson pre-folded watercolor cards. Copy and cut out faces and necks for cards. Draw shirts. Cut out newspaper and paint with Titan Buff for blouse.Use different patterns and colors of papers or fabrics for boat and pants. Arrange as desired and glue to card. Use tissue for water. Paint as desired. Once paint is dry, add line drawing with fine tip nib to finish characters on card. Use Paper Shaper scissors along bottom edge to create design.

I was excited to do a few cards for this project. The whimsical themes are well suited for just about any occasion. Claudine

Don't worry little 'poppet', everything is going to be OK.

Claudine

Girl in Boat
Card

Boy with Bird
Card

The text on the journal cover reads:

W Things I Wish Someone Had Told ME In my youth AND OTHER Thoughts of Wisdom...

Instructions Page 42

Wisdom Journal Roben-Marie Smith

> "When I set out to create my Wisdom Journal, I was not only thinking about the many **words of wisdom** that were bestowed upon me when I was growing up, but also the mysteries of life left for me to discover on my own. This layout expresses my **thoughts** and **feelings** about both."
>
> Roben-Marie

Roben-Marie Smith is a mixed media, collage and book artist and owner of Paperbag Studios, a company that features collage materials and a line of rubber stamps, including alphabets, vintage photos, ephemera and some of Roben-Marie's own designs. Roben-Marie is also a full-time instructor who travels nationally, sharing her passion for creating art through teaching others. She resides in Florida with her husband, Bobby who is very supportive and assists her in the business. In addtition to TweetyJill Publications titles, her work has been published in *Somerset Studio, Stamper's Sampler, Legacy, PLAY Zine, ARTitude Zine, Altered Books 101* by Design Originals and the 2004 Somerset Studio Art Journal Calender.

Roben-Marie writes: "As I look back on my life I can see the early signs of a creative person trying to find her niche. I tried every creative outlet I could find; I even made my own stuffed animals. I dabbled in batik, carved my own stamps, made canvas rugs and my own Christmas ornaments. I had a few awards under my belt for collage and drawing, and my parents continued to oblige me in my endeavors. They encouraged and supported me. They knew one day I would find my calling.

Finally in 1997, while living in North Carolina, I was introduced to scrapbooking. A short time later I discovered rubber stamping and knew I was hooked! I moved to Florida, where a wonderful artsy stamp store opened in town, and my love of rubber stamping, collage and book arts began. I attended conventions and read every book I could get my hands on to teach myself this new found art. Before long, I began teaching.

Today I feel that I have finally found my inspiration. I love anything vintage, although I have been trying to challenge myself to reach beyond my comfort zone and try new things. Sometimes I find it a challenge to make art because I enjoy looking at and tinkering with my supplies so much. I am like a kid after trick or treating who lays all her candy on the floor to look at it. I love to look at my supplies and trinkets almost as much as creating art with them.

I feel blessed to be doing something that I enjoy so much and I look forward to what lies ahead. My mom used to say 'Anything worth having is worth waiting for.' I think she was right. It took long enough to find something I truly love and it has been well worth the wait!"

Wisdom Journal: Cover pg 40

Materials:

Gated Journal: 7gypsies

Script and Text Papers: 7gypsies

Large and Small Tags: Local Craft Store

Transparency Film: Local Office Supply

Walnut Ink Crystals: Stamper's Anonymous

Antique Ivory Acrylic Paint: Delta

Black Adirondack Dye Inkpad: Ranger Industries

Small Children Rubber Stamp: Limited Edition Rubber Stamps

Old Script Writing Rubber Stamp: Hero Arts

Mesh Paper: Magenta

Solid Ribbon: Local Craft Store

Checked Ribbon: Offray

Printed and Blank Twill: 7gypsies

Twine and Beads: Local Craft Store

Bull Dog Clip: Local Office Supply

Black Nail Head, Alligator Clip and Metal Alphabet Charms: 7gypsies

Square Metal Brad: Making Memories

Adhesives: UHU Glue Stick; Glue Dots International; Judi Kins Diamond Glaze

Other: Cardboard

Tools: Marvy Uchida Embossing Heat Tool and spray bottle

Instructions:

1. Detach covers from book and paint both sides with two coats of Antique Ivory paint; let dry. Combine water with walnut ink crystals in spray bottle. Spritz both sides of book covers until desired look is achieved. Heat set if desired or let air-dry.

2. Tear and glue papers to covers. Add square brad to cardboard piece and glue to cover. Using Diamond Glaze, attach printed transparency to cover. Wrap twill around left cover and connect with nail head. Glue mesh paper to cover with glue stick and wrap twill around cove and tie off with beads and alligator clip.

3. Spritz tags with walnut ink and wrap largest tag over the top of the right side of cover. Add bulldog clip and "month" twill piece. Adhere metal alphabet charms to cover with Glue Dots.

4. Once book is reassembled, tie solid ribbons, twine and checkered ribbon to the left-hand side coils.

5. Stamp script and children stamps with black dye inkpad to one side of small tags. Glue printed twill to the other side. Tie to ribbons on left side of book.

> *" I wish someone had told me when I was younger to begin a journal and add to it often."*
>
> Roben-Marie

Wisdom Journal: #2

Materials:

Alphabet and Word Papers: 7gypsies

Brown Paper: Paper Cuts

Defined Words: Making Memories

Medium Manila Tag: Local Office Supply

Black Adirondack Dye Inkpad: Ranger Industries

Black Crayola Crayon: Local Craft or Office Supply

Date Stamper: Local Office Supply

Printed Twill and Black Paper Tab Holder: 7gypsies

Twine: Local Craft Store

Mini Brads: Making Memories

Adhesive: UHU Glue Stick

Tools: Fiskars 1/8" Hole Punch and Small Rectangle Punch, spray bottle and silky sponge

Instructions:

1. (Left): Tear and glue Word Paper and Defined Word to inside cover board. Draw over with black crayon. (Twine and twill are wrapped around from journal cover instructions.)

2. (Middle): Tear and glue Alphabet paper to page. Computer-generate words and print onto brown text paper. Tear, sponge edges with black ink and glue to page with glue stick.

3. Glue "what" twill to inside of folded paper tab. Place tab on page and attach with mini brads with 1/8" hole punch. Glue page to next page to follow. Punch holes with rectangle punch and add twine.

4. (Right): Spritz Word paper and manila tag with walnut ink crystals dissolved in water. Glue paper to cover and add Defined Words; highlight with black crayon. Add twine and staples to tag. Imprint date with date stamper and black dye ink. Glue to inside cover board.

Wisdom Journal: #3

Materials:

Green Paper: Anna Griffin

Cardstock: Local Craft Store

Spiral Easel: 7gypsies

Ribbon, Fabric and Lace Flower: Local Craft Store

Adhesives: UHU Glue Stick; Glue Dots International

Instructions:

Cut and glue green paper to page. Adhere lace flower with glue dot. Cut and fringe the edges of fabric and glue to page. Using ribbon, attach the spiral easel to the page. Computer-generate words onto cardstock and cut out. Place word cards into slits in the spiral easel.

Wisdom Journal: #4

Materials:

Script and Patterned Papers: 7gypsies

Black Paper: Local Craft Store or Office Supply

Black Adirondack Dye Inkpad: Ranger Industries

Sharpie Black Fine Point Marker: Sanford

Alphabet Stamps: MaVinci's Reliquary

Twine: Local Craft Store

Metal "In and Out" and Gold Spine: 7gypsies

Eyelets: Making Memories

Adhesive: UHU Glue Stick

Tools: American Tag Eyelet Setter and Fiskars 1/8" Hole Punch and Small Square Punch

Instructions:

1. Tear and glue black and printed text paper to page. Re-punch covered holes using small square punch.

2. Use alphabet stamps to highlight words. Journal with black Sharpie pen.

3. Add "In and Out" to gold spine bar. Add eyelets to page and tie twine through and around bar to hold in place.

Wisdom Journal: #5

Materials:

White Computer Paper: Local Office Supply

Adhesive: UHU Glue Stick

Instructions:

1. Computer-generate words "Honesty, Kindness and Flexibility" in software program and run journal page through printer.

2. Computer-generate words and print onto plain paper. Cut out and glue to page with glue stick. Cut patterned scrapbook paper into three squares and glue to page at bottom.

Wisdom Journal: #6

Instructions:

Word Paper: 7gypsies

Coin Tag: Local Office Supply

Silver Heart Clip: Making Memories

Adhesives: UHU Glue Stick; Glue Dots International

Other: Black and white photo

Instructions:

Glue photo to page. Cut Word paper into strips and glue to page, framing the photo. Pull one paper strip through the heart clip prior to gluing to page. Cut out "words" from Word paper and glue to coin tag. Adhere coin tag to page with Glue Dot.

Wisdom Journal: #7

Materials:

Green Paper: Anna Griffin

Lace Flower: Local Craft Store

Silver Mini Brads: Making Memories

Black Photo Turns: 7gypsies

Adhesives: UHU Glue Stick and Glue Dots International

Other: Black and white photo

Tools: Fiskars 1/8 " Hole Punch

Instructions:

Cut and glue green paper to page. Adhere lace flowers with Glue Dot. Cut and glue black and white photo to page. Computer-generate words and print in color; glue to page. Punch holes with 1/8" hole punch at corners and add photo turns with mini brads.

Wisdom Journal: #8

Materials:

"Laugh" definition from dictionary

Instructions:

Scan "Laugh" dictionary definition into computer; enlarge and print onto journal page.

Wisdom Journal: #9

Materials:

Script and Patterned Papers: 7gypsies

Green Cardstock: Paper Cuts

Sharpie Black Fine Point Marker: Sanford

Small Jewelry Tag: Local Craft Store or Office Supply

Printed Twill and Bamboo Clips: 7gypsies

Adhesive: UHU Glue Stick

Other: Fabric, safety pin and photo

Instructions:

Tear and glue script paper and green paper and glue to page. Tear photograph edges and glue to page. Trim fabric piece and twill to size and connect with safety pin and glue to page. Use marker to write "mom" on small tag and glue to page. Add bamboo clips.

My mom showed me kindness and was always honest. These qualities are very important to me, and as I have grown older, I have found that flexibility is another important trait. Thanks, Mom, for being such a great role model.

Roben-Marie

Wisdom Journal: #10

Materials:

White Computer Paper: Local Office Supply

Coin Tags: American Tag or Local Office Supply

Walnut Ink Crystals: Anima Designs

Black Adirondack Dye Inkpad: Ranger Industries

Sharpie Black Fine Point Marker: Sanford

Script Text Rubber Stamp: Hero Arts

Ribbon and Twine: Local Craft Store

Adhesives: UHU Glue Stick; Glue Dots International; Clear Scotch Tape

Tools: Spray bottle

Instructions:

Using black dye ink and script stamp, stamp the background of page. Spritz white paper, manila tag and five coin tags with walnut ink crystals dissolved in water. Tear paper and glue to page. Place two pieces of brown ribbon across page and tape to back. Tie twine to coin tags and adhere to page with Glue Dots. Write various words to tags with black marker.

Wisdom Journal: #11

Materials:

Scrapbook Paper: 7gypsies

White Computer Paper: Local Office Supply

Bamboo Clips: 7gypsies

Adhesive: UHU Glue Stick

Instructions:

Tear and glue scrapbook paper to page. Computer-generate colored text, cul out and glue to page. Add bamboo clips to top of page.

Wisdom Journal: #12

Materials:

White Computer Paper: Local Office Supply

Black Crayola Crayon: Local Craft Store

Twine: Local Craft Store

Adhesive: UHU Glue Stick

Tools: Fiskars Rectangle Hole Punch

Instructions:

Cut and glue computer-generated words to page. Outline words with black crayon. Glue page to next page in book. Punch three holes in the right side of page and add twine.

Dare to Dream Scrapbook page

Roben-Marie Smith

Materials:

Floral Paper: K&Company

Rub-On Words: Making Memories

FoofaBets: FoofaLa

Small White Tags: Local Office Supply

White and Pink Acrylic Paint: Delta

Black StazOn Solvent Inkpad: Tsukineko

"Numbers" Rubber Stamp: Paperbag Studios

Date Stamper: Office Supply Store or Local Craft Store

Pink Velvet Ribbon: FoofaLa

Lace, Silk Flowers and Ribbon: Local Craft Store

Velvet Leaves: ARTchix Studio

White Nail Heads: 7gypsies

Silver Mini Brads and Large Ribbon Charm: Making Memories

Adhesives: UHU Glue Stick; Glue Dots International

Other: Old text papers and vintage buttons

Tools: Stapler and small paintbrush

Instructions:

Glue ribbon and photo to page. Add a ribbon charm to one ribbon prior to adding to page. Add white and pink acrylic paint to old text papers, "ME" FoofaBets and a tag. Add date and ribbon to tag and glue to page. Glue FoofaBets to page above tag. Add mini brads and nail heads to silk flowers. Glue flowers and velvet leaves to page.

Using black dye inkpad, stamp "Numbers" onto a small tag and glue to page. Add rub-on words "Dare to Dream" to page. Using Glue Dots, adhere vintage buttons to pink velvet ribbon.

"I just love this mini spiral journal. The photograph of the little girl *inspired* one of my new rubber stamp designs, so I chose to use the *original* for this journal. I imagine she is sitting for her school picture. She appears so happy, and it is so unusual to find vintage images where people are actually smiling!"

Roben-Marie

Dream Mini-Journal Roben-Marie Smith

Materials:

Mini Journal: 7gypsies

Scrapbook Paper: Li'l Davis Designs

Sticker Words: Pebbles, Inc.

Defined Words: Making Memories

Acrylic Paint: Delta

Pitch Black Adirondack Inkpad: Ranger Industries

"No. 451921" Rubber Stamp: Paperbag Studios

Ribbon: Offray

Twine and Silk Flower: Local Craft Store

Silver Mini Brad and Ribbon Charm: Making Memories

Adhesives: UHU Glue Stick; Glue Dots International

Other: Vintage buttons

Tools: Small paintbrush

Instructions

Disassemble book and cover front and back cover boards with scrapbook paper. Cut Defined Words and vintage photo and layer to front of book. Using a dry-brush technique, add pink acrylic paint to the front cover. Stamp "No. 451921" with black dye ink to bottom left corner of cover. Adhere ribbon charm to ribbon and add to cover with Glue Dots. Add a mini brad to the center of a silk flower and glue to cover. Adhere buttons with Glue Dots and sticker word to cover. Reassemble book and tie ribbons and twine to the coil spine.

Three Sisters
Vintage Journal
Roben-Marie Smith

Materials:

Children's Book: Local Discount Store

Brown Envelopes: Local Office Supply

Brown Scrapbook Paper: Scrap Ease

Handmade Brown Paper: Black Ink

Parchment Paper: Local Office Supply

Expresso Adirondack Inkpad: Ranger Industries

"Fragments" Definition Rubber Stamp: A Lost Art

Mica Tile: USArtQuest

Ribbon and Button: Local Craft Store

Wax Thread: Stamper's Anonymous

Eyelets: Making Memories

Adhesives: UHU Glue Stick; Glue Dots International; Judi Kins Diamond Glaze; Scotch Clear Tape

Other: Dictionary page, vintage photos, coffee-stained paper and vintage key plate

Tools: American Tag Eyelet Setter; Fiskars 1/8" Circle Punch; Carl MFG. Co., LTD 1/2" Circle Punch and Making Memories Sewing Needle

Instructions:

Cover and Book: Remove the pages from a children's book and cover with handmade paper. Fold various sizes of parchment paper and coffee-stained paper together and sew into book with wax thread. Add a button to the outside of the spine and thread the ends of the thread through it and tie off.

Layer vintage photo to cut pieces of dictionary page and scrapbook papers. Add a small amount of Diamond Glaze to a piece of mica and adhere to top of photo. Punch holes in photo and add eyelets. Pull ribbons through holes and tape to back of papers. Glue to page. Using Glue Dots, adhere vintage key plate to front of book.

Inside View One: Punch two 1/2" circles out of coffee-stained paper. Use eyelets and a string to create a string button closure on two brown envelopes. Glue one to the inside cover and the other to the inside back.

" I discovered this beautiful handmade paper and knew that I would create a vintage journal with it. The photograph of the three women was found at a flea market and is the journal's namesake. It took several months to design this journal with all of its folds, pockets and various size pages. Of all the classes I teach, the "Three Sisters Vintage Journal" class is the most popular to date. " Roben-Marie

Three Sisters Vintage Journal Inside

So closely interwoven have been our lives, our purposes, and experiences that, separated, we have a feeling of incompleteness—united, such strength of self-association that no ordinary obstacles, difficulties, or dangers ever appear to us insurmountable.

-Elizabeth Cady Stanton

The WriterCard Roben-Marie Smith

Materials:

Striped Paper: K&Company

Library Card: ARTchix Studio

Green Card Stock: Canson

"Little One" Transparency: ARTchix Studio

Pitch Black Adirondack Inkpad: Ranger Industries

"No. 1" Rubber Stamp: Treasure Cay

Silk Flower: Local Craft Store

Metal Alphabet Charms, Decorative Brad, Staple and Ribbon Charm: Making Memories

Adhesives: UHU Glue Stick; Glue Dots International

Other: Lace and old number paper

Instructions:

Tear and glue old number paper and scrapbook paper to card front. Staple transparency to library card and glue to card front. Adhere lace with ribbon charm and metal alphabets to card front with Glue Dots. Add a decorative brad to the center of a silk flower and glue to card front.

*I was having a **creative block** the day I designed 'The Writer' card. I chose this image because I viewed this little girl as perhaps having writer's block or maybe just **seeking inspiration** for her next word or phrase.* Roben-Marie

Materials:

Black Text Paper: 7gypsies

Old Postcard Paper: K&Company

Cream Cardstock: Local Office Supply

Sticker Word: Pebbles, Inc.

Poemstone: Sonnets by Creative Imaginations

Definition Words: FoofaLa

Manila Tags and Small Jewelry Tags:
Local Office Supply

White Acrylic Paint: Delta

Pesto Adirondack Inkpad: Ranger Industries

**Metal Alphabet Charms, Decorative Brad
and Stickpin:** Making Memories

Safety Pins: Li'l Davis Designs

Printed Twill: 7gypsies

Velvet Leaf: ARTchix Studio

Silk Flower and Ribbon: Local Craft Store

Adhesives: UHU Glue Stick; Glue Dots International

Other: Vintage button, old lace and book

Tools: Stapler and silk sponge

Instructions:

Remove the pages from an old book and cover the inside with old postcard paper. Using a dry brush, add white paint very sparingly to outside covers (keep brush as dry as possible during application to allow green color to show through). Cut cardstock and fold to fit into book for pages. Secure pages into the book by tying them in with ribbon. Ribbon should be tied on the outside at the spine. Using safety pins, add small jewelry tags to ribbon on spine. Write on the tags as desired.

Layer pieces of scrapbook paper, definition and old photo to cover with glue stick. Add a decorative brad to the center of a silk flower and a stickpin to a velvet leaf. Adhere both to cover with Glue Dots. Adhere metal alphabet charms, vintage lace and buttons to cover with Glue Dots.

Wrinkle and sponge four manila tags with Pesto dye ink. Tear each tag and glue the edge to random pages in the book. Be sure that part of the tag shows out of the side of the book. On the first tag, staple a scrap of the old postcard paper. On the second tag, add a sticker word. On the third tag, add a piece of printed twill and on the last tag, add a Poemstone.

Chereb Eyes
Journal Roben-Marie Smith

cher-ub (cher´ub), n. [pl. cherubs (´ubz, cherubim (´oo-bim)], an angel to a seraphin in rank; a beautiful child [pl. cherubs].

The sweet little girl in this picture is my niece. Charlie. *It was easy to be inspired by this* cherub face! *She adorns the cover of a book I found at a flea market. I removed the pages and added new ones with ribbons. This is a great way to create a journal while recycling an old book!* Roben-Marie

Remember Roben-Marie Smith
Journal

Materials:

Small Spiral Bound Tag Journal: 7gypsies

Green Printed Paper: Anna Griffin

Postcard Collage Paper: K&Company

Vintage Collage Image: ARTchix Studio

Black Acrylic Paint: Delta

Ribbon: Offray

Printed Twill: 7gypsies

Twine, Silk Flower and Buttons: Local Craft Store

Black Metal File Tab: Paperbag Studios

Metal Word Charm Tag: K&Company

Silver Mini Brad: Making Memories

Silver Eyelets: Dritz

Adhesives: UHU Glue Stick; Glue Dots International

Tools: Eyelet setter and small paint brush

Instructions:

Layer torn scrapbook paper to front and back covers. Add vintage photo to front cover. Dry-brush the covers with black acrylic paint. Attach silver eyelets to the metal tab and glue printed twill to the inside. Punch holes into cover for placement and attach with twine. Wrap ribbon around cover and tie at front. Add a silver mini brad to the center of a silk flower. Adhere flower, leaf, buttons and metal word tag to the cover with Glue Dots. Tie a variety of ribbon and twine to the coil bind at the top.

This may seem a little odd, but I found these great metal file tabs and wanted to use one of them in a project. My 'Remember' journal was basically designed around this black metal tab! Roben-Marie

Journey
Journal
Roben-Marie Smith

"I have a lot of old vintage photos in my collection, including the ones that come in tri-fold holders. I decided one day to make a journal out of one and the "Journey" journal was created. This is such an easy way to transform these holders. They come in all kinds of sizes and make awesome gifts!" Roben-Marie

Materials:

Floral and Ledger Papers: K&Company

Vellum: EK Success

Vintage Postcard Collage Image: Paperbag Studios

Parchment Paper: Local Office Supply

Library Card: ARTchix Studio

Alphabet Letters: FoofaLa

Defined Words: Making Memories

Simply Stated Word Rub-Ons: Making Memories

Word Sticker: Pebbles, Inc.

Tags: Local Craft Store

Olive Green Acrylic Paint: Liquitex

Black Adirondack Inkpad: Ranger Industries

Date Stamper: Local Office Supply

Silk Leaves: ARTchix Studio

Beads, Silk Flower and Ribbon: Local Craft Store

Wax Thread: Stamper's Anonymous

Metal Alphabet Charms, Decorative Brad, T-Pin and Staples: Making Memories

Bulldog Clip: Local Office Supply

Adhesives: UHU Glue Stick; Glue Dots International

Other: Vintage buttons and photo holder

Tools: Stapler; 1/8" Hole Punch by Fiskars and small paintbrush

Instructions:

Layer torn and cut scrapbook papers to the outside and inside of a vintage photo holder. Add a vintage collage image to the front cover. Wrinkle and paint a small tag with olive acrylic paint. Glue to cover and add bulldog clip with button to secure. Add beads to the string and scrap paper, leaf, mini tag and word to the tag with a staple. Add rub-on word to the front of the journal.

Attach a decorative brad to the center of a silk flower; glue silk leaves and flower to cover flap. Add small beads to a stickpin and add to leaf. Attach a small tag with the date written on it.

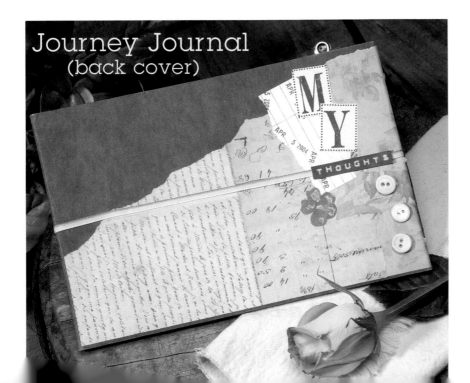

Journey Journal
(back cover)

On the back cover, add library card stamped with the date, paper letters and sticker word. Make sure the closure ribbon wraps around and is glued under the sticker word. Adhere buttons with Glue Dots. Bring ribbon around the front and glue a small piece under the silk flower to hold it into place.

Fold several pieces of paper and a piece of floral vellum. Sew into the fold of the photo holder on the inside to create the journal pages. Adhere metal number charms to the inside cover with Glue Dots.

Nana's Memories Keepsake Book
Patti Muma

Patti Muma is a self-taught artist who began creating scrapbooks eight years ago and then expanded to tag art, artist trading cards, altered books, hand-bound books and greeting cards. Her work has been featured in numerous zines, including *Pumpkin Creek Zine*, *Off The Shelf Zine*, *Winter Solstice Zine* and most recently, *Collage Cats 2nd Anniversery Zine*. She is a member of several on-line artist groups and lives in Vicksburg, Michigan.

Patti writes: "I have always had an addiction to all things paper. As a child, I created collages for my bedroom walls using magazine clippings and album covers. As a pre-school teacher, I relied on art to entertain and educate three and four year old children. As a mom, scrapbooking was a natural extension of my art and the love I have of family life.

In 2002, my scrapbook space that existed in the corner of the family room became my workshop, which I call "Basement Dweller Design." The family room furniture found a new room and the scrapbook and rubberstamp supplies expanded to an official art studio. A local scrapbook shop has featured my tags and a gift shop in town carries my embellished journals, collage tag art and hand-bound notebooks.

When not in the studio, I am busy with my very supportive husband of seventeen years, Bob, and our four great kids. I also work full-time at our local hospital as a patient care assistant."

Treasures from the past can come to us in many forms, but none can be as precious as memories. Ancestors can reach through the years to teach us, to guide us and to remind us we are not so very different after all. Patti

Nana's Memories Keepsake Book pg 54

Materials:

"Script," "Advertisme" and "Measurement" Papers: 7gypsies

Tan Cardstock: Local Craft Store

Manilla Folder: Local Office Supply

Buttons and Borders Sticker: Life's Journey by K&Company

Oval Bubble Phrase: Li'l Davis Design

Tags: Hand-Cut by Artist

Craft-Colored Slide Mount: Limited Editions

Sepia Archival Inkpad: Ranger Industries

Brown, Ochre and Terra Cotta Inkpads: Marvy Matchables

Walnut Ink: Postmodern Design

Tiny Typewriter Letters Rubber Stamp: Hero Arts

Ribbon: Offray

Scrabble Letter Tiles: Limited Editions

Watch Charm: 7gypsies

Scissors Charm: Jolee's by You

Metal Oval Disk: Li'l Davis Designs

Nickel and Brass Brads: Local Craft Store

Label Holder and Standard Size Brad: Local Craft Store or Office Supply

Nickel Eyelet: Making Memories

Black Snaps: Dritz

Adhesives: Avery Glue Stick; Artsy Collage Gel; Pioneer Photo Mount Squares; Super Bond Glue

Other: Composition book, paper doily, wooden buttons, green fiber, piece of old sewing pattern, scanned and copied vintage dictionary page and vintage photo

Tools: Paper cutter, scissors, craft knife, sandpaper, wax paper, sponge for inks, old plastic gift card (for spreading glue), small wallpaper roller and awl

Instructions:

Stain manila folder with walnut stain, allow to dry. Cut tag from folder (6 °" x 3 1/16"). Adhere sewing pattern piece to left side of tag with glue stick; trim off excess. Attach Measurement paper along left and bottom edge. Attach vintage photo to walnut-stained slide mount. Adhere slide mount with glue stick. Attach scrabble letters to tape measure area of tag.

For small tag, stain tan cardstock with walnut stain; allow to dry. Computer-generate "A stitch in time…" onto walnut-stained cardstock, then cut a tag from paper around the phrase; sponge edge with brown ink. Add eyelet and fiber. Attach small tag to larger one. Attach sewing notions and charms using super bond glue. Add ribbon and then set tag aside.

To cover composition book, begin by sanding cover to remove gloss; wipe with paper towel. Place wax paper between first page and front cover. Apply small amount of collage gel to cover and spread evenly with plastic card. Place chosen cover paper onto glue and press out wrinkles and air bubbles. Use wallpaper roller (or bone folder) to smooth out paper and to adhere paper firmly to cover. Repeat to back side of book. (The book may require pressing to prevent curling of covers.) Wrap book in wax paper and press between heavier books for 24 hours. When dry, trim paper along the cover with a craft knife.

Sponge both front and back covers with the various inks listed for an aged effect. Sponge around very edge of covers with sepia ink. Using glue stick, adhere doily to upper left-hand corner and trim off excess with craft knife. Adhere sewing machine ad from Advertisement paper to lower left-hand corner. Add border sticker along side black border, press firmly. Add large tag (made earlier) to right hand side of book. Use photo mounts to attach metal oval frame onto doily; place Bubble Phrase in frame.

Using the vintage dictionary page scanned earlier, cut the definition of "ancestor" to fit label holder. Place inside holder and secure with a small piece of tape on back. Using awl, puncture front cover and attach label holder with brass brads.

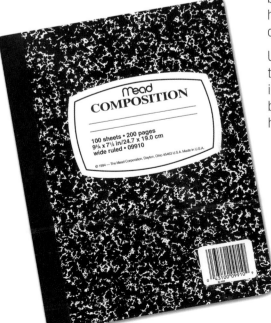

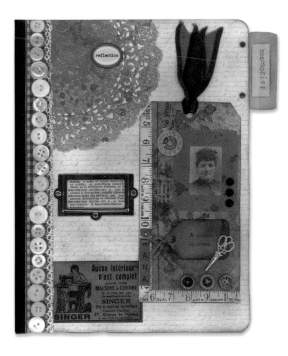

To make index on right-hand side of front cover, cut a piece of tan cardstock 2" x 4" and fold. Cut open end at an angle. Cut small "window" into one side of folded index; sponge with inks. On scrap piece of paper, use stamps to write "memories." Place this in window of index and adhere with glue stick. Use awl to puncture front cover and attach the index using nickel-colored brads.

To make ribbon place-marker, stamp words onto ribbon using letter stamps and brown ink. To attach to book, use awl to puncture the top of the back cover's inside corner. Clip a standard brad through this hole from the outside of book. Punch the end of ribbon, printed side down, onto brad. Open wings of brad to secure. Flip book over, running ribbon to front of the book.

These precious journals are anyone's idea of a treasured gift and will brighten the days of all who receive them. See how simple it is to convert dollar store composition notebooks into works of art. Blank journals are intimate gifts, allowing room for one to express their individual thoughts, ideas, reflections and more. A hand-made journal seems even more meaningful; as the gift literally shares a small piece of its creator to joyfully speak to the one who receives it. Patti

Materials:

Black and Tan Cardstock and Batik Background Paper: Local Craft Store

Printer Paper: Local Office Supply

"Postcards and Letters" Collage Sheet: ARTchix Studio

Brown Typeset Letters: Nostalgiques by Rebecca Sower/EK Success

Sepia Archival Inkpad: Ranger Industries

Brown Inkpad: Marvy Matchables

Walnut Ink: Postmodern Design

Printed Twill: 7gypsies

Brads: Local Craft Store

Adhesives: Avery Glue Stick; Artsy Collage Gel; Pioneer Photo Mount Corners

Other: Composition book and copy of vintage photo

Tools: Paper cutter, craft knife, scissors, sponge for inks, sandpaper, wax paper, old plastic gift card (for spreading glue), small wallpaper roller and awl

IInstructions:

Lightly sand composition book to remove gloss; wipe with paper towel. Place wax paper between first page and front cover. Apply small amount of collage gel to front cover and spread evenly with plastic card. Place chosen cover paper onto glue and press out wrinkles and air bubbles. Use wallpaper roller (or bone folder) to smooth out paper and to adhere paper firmly to cover. Repeat to back side of book. (The book may require pressing to prevent curling of covers.) Wrap book in wax paper and press between heavier books for 24 hours. When dry, trim paper along cover with craft knife.

Stain tan cardstock with walnut ink and allow to dry. Type the words "dream," "discover," and "truth" and also create a text box in rust color. Inside text box, in white letters, type the word "journal." Print these words onto the walnut-stained tan cardstock. Cut out words and sponge edges lightly with brown ink. Tear text box edges and then sponge edges using sepia ink. Using standard printer paper, type the phrase for title and print. Tear this title out and sponge edges lightly with sepia ink.

Tear edges of photo, sponge lightly with brown ink and mat onto black cardstock. Attach brads to each corner of matted photo. Cut out small postcard from ArtChix collage sheet.

Glue all of the prepared elements onto the front of journal using Avery Glue Stick. Place a photo mount square to the back of matted photo in each corner for extra support. Place typeset letters over photo to spell "FAITH".

To attach place marker, use an awl to puncture back cover. Slip standard size brad through this hole, from the outside of book. Punch an end of printed twill (print side down) over the brad. Open wings of brad to secure. Flip book over, running twill to the front of the book.

Vintage Journal
Unexamined Life Patti Muma

The unexamined life is not worth living...
-Socrates

Discover

F A I T H

Journal

Truth

Dream

This journal features one of my favorite quotes. I have always kept a journal, reflecting on the changes and growth that life inevitably brings. Examine, remember and cherish your life with words. Patti

Materials:

Terre Brun Paper: 7gypsies

Tan Cardstock: Local Craft Store

Dictionary Paper: K&Company

"Measure" Sticker: Nostalgiques by Rebecca Sower/EK Success

Adhesive Photo Corners: Local Craft Store

Slide Mount: Design Originals

Brown Inkpad: Marvy Matchables

Walnut Ink: Postmodern Design

Caramel-Colored Ribbon: Offray

Adhesives: Avery Glue Stick; Artsy Collage Gel; Pioneer Photo Mount Squares; Super Bond Glue

Other: Composition book, copy of chosen photo, old key and standard size brad.

Tools: Paper cutter, craft knife, scissors, sandpaper, wax paper, sponge for inks, old plastic gift card (for spreading glue), small wallpaper roller and awl

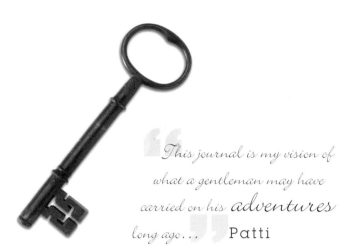

This journal is my vision of what a gentleman may have carried on his adventures long ago... Patti

Instructions:

Lightly sand composition book to remove gloss. Wipe with paper towel. Place wax paper between first page and front cover. Apply small amount of collage gel to front cover and spread evenly with plastic card. Place chosen cover paper onto glue and press out wrinkles and air bubbles. Use wallpaper roller (or bone folder) to smooth out paper and to adhere paper firmly to cover. Repeat on back side of book. (The book may require pressing to prevent curling of covers.) Wrap book in wax paper and press between heavier books for 24 hours. When dry, trim paper along cover with craft knife.

Using walnut ink, stain tan cardstock and slide mount; allow to dry. Type phrase in all caps: "I AM THE MASTER OF MY FATE" then create a text box and fill with rust color. Type inside text box, in a white font, (all caps) "I AM THE CAPTAIN OF MY SOUL." Print out onto the walnut-stained cardstock.

Cut these phrases out and set aside. With remaining stained cardstock, mat picture. Sponge photo corners with brown ink and placed onto matted photo.

Place "Measure" sticker along side of black border on front of book. Attach matted photo with photo mounts and glue stick. Glue phrases on top and along side of photo. Cut out the definition of "journey" from dictionary paper and place inside walnut-stained slide mount. Attach both slide mount and key to book with super bond glue for added strength.

To attach ribbon place marker, use awl to puncture the top of back cover. Slip standard size brad through this hole, from the outside of the book. Punch an end of the ribbon over brad. Open wings of the brad to secure. Flip book over, running ribbon to the front of the book.

Journals aren't just pretty notebooks for women to keep their sentiments in. The versatility of art allows for creating sophisticated notebooks for the men in your life too. Put one in his den and watch the small pieces of paper with phone numbers and notes scratched with each day's goings on disappear into an organized and maybe even dated notebook. Patti

Masculine Journal
Patti Muma

You can count
on me.

always

take

the

gentle

path

"I love creating these little books! Perfect for hostess gifts, birthdays (for all ages), Mother's Day, Father's Day and "just because," they are also great for to-do, to-go and to-get lists as well as on the spot storage for phone numbers and email adresses. I try to keep a few of these books in my studio, ready to embellish. In a short amount of time, I am able to create a "little bit of art" and at the same time create a small supply of last minute gifts to always have on hand!" Patti

You Can Count On Me Patti Muma
Mini-Composition Notebook

Materials:

"Calendre" Paper: 7gypsies

Printer Paper: Local Office Supply

Vintage Image: Somerset Studios Collage Clips

Brown, Ochre and Terra Cotta Inkpads: Marvy Matchables

Leaf Green Inkpad: Ancient Page by Clearsnap

Adhesives: Avery Glue Stick, Artsy Collage Gel

Other: Mini-sized composition book, brown craft paper and copy of vintage bingo card

Tools: Paper cutter, sandpaper, wax paper, sponge for inks, old plastic gift card (for spreading glue) wallpaper roller, ruler and craft knife

Instructions:

Lightly sand mini-composition book to remove gloss. Wipe with paper towel. Place wax paper between first page and front cover. Apply small amount of collage gel to front cover and spread evenly with plastic card. Place chosen cover paper onto glue and press out wrinkles and air bubbles. Use small wallpaper roller (or bone folder) to smooth paper and to adhere paper to cover firmly. Repeat on back side of book. (The book may need to be pressed to prevent curling.) Wrap book in wax paper and press between heavier books for 24 hours. When paper is dry, trim around cover with craft knife.

Measure and tear "Calendre" paper to fit as border on front cover. Sponge brown ink onto torn edge. Glue along binding with glue stick. Tear picture to fit cover, sponge ink to torn edge and glue onto cover with glue stick.

Computer-generate "You can count on me" onto standard printer paper; tear to fit front cover. Sponge lightly with cocoa ink on front as well as along torn edges. Adhere to front cover with glue stick.

Cut individual number squares from copy of vintage bingo card. Use direct-to-paper method to color squares using various colors of inks. Adhere to back cover with glue stick.

Take The Gentle Path Patti Muma
Mini-Composition Notebook

Materials:

Lace Background Paper and Black Cardstock: Local Craft Store

Collage Sheet: ARTchix Studio

Printer Paper: Local Office Supply

Domed Torn Paper Words: Life's Journey by K&Company

Sepia Archival Inkpad: Ranger Industries

Adhesives: Avery Glue Stick; Artsy Collage Gel

Other: Small sized composition book

Tools: Paper cutter, scissors, sandpaper, wax paper, old plastic gift card (for spreading glue), sponge for ink, wallpaper roller, ruler and craft knife

Instructions:

Lightly sand mini-composition book to remove gloss; wipe with paper towel. Place wax paper between first page and front cover. Apply small amount of collage gel to front cover and spread evenly with plastic card. Place chosen cover paper onto glue and press out wrinkles and air bubbles. Use small wallpaper roller (or bone folder) to smooth out paper and to adhere paper firmly to cover. Repeat on back side of book. (The book may require pressing to prevent curling of covers.) Wrap the book in wax paper and press between heavier books for 24 hours. When dry, trim paper along cover with craft knife.

Cut pictures from ARTchix collage sheet. Mat pictures onto black cardstock. Adhere to cover with glue stick. Glue a picture on both front and back of book.

Computer-generate "take the gentle path" onto standard printer paper. Be sure space words far enough apart to allow cutting out the words separately. Cut out words and sponge lightly with sepia ink.

Use glue stick to adhere words onto front cover, along side of picture. Adhere the word "always" along the top of the front cover. Sponge edges of cover lightly with sepia ink to give the book an aged effect.

A Swing
Kim Henkel
Scrapbook Page

Journaling on the scrapbook page reads:

NAME Susan Lanette Robinson

BOX NUMBERS 1 2 3 4 6

How do U like to go up in A SWING up in the air so BLUE? OH I think it's the pleasantest thing ever a child can do

FIFTY FLAGS

JENNY SARGS ALPHABET

RAIN AND SHINE

ROUND

99 100 101

1956

> "This photo is of my mom in 1956. Having a swing all to herself was a hard feat when she was one of five siblings! I wanted to create whimsical journaling using several of my favorite stamps and stickers." Kim

Kim Henkel has only been scrapbooking for two years, yet her work appears in a number of publications, including *Simple Scrapbooks*, *Legacy* magazine and *Memory Makers* magazine. She is also a design team member for FoofaLa. As a child Kim loved paper, and later developed a passion for fabric. She earned a degree in Fashion Merchandising, and made quilts for many years. One fateful day she taught a friend to quilt, who in turn, introduced Kim to scrapbooking. Now Kim enjoys working with two of her favorite elements — paper and fabric — to create her beautiful handmade cards, journals and scrapbook pages.

Kim Writes: "One of my earliest childhood memories is watching my mom sew Raggedy Ann dolls and making my Halloween costumes. She always made everything with 'SEW' much love!

Besides having a fascination with paper ... paper dolls, stationary, coloring books and stickers, I started to have an interest in fabric and anything handmade. I remember trying to use my mom's sewing machine and breaking it on more than one occasion.

As an adult, I bought a professional sewing machine and began making quilts, lots of quilts of all sizes. After making quilts for 12 years, I ended up with two cabinets filled with my favorite fabrics. I finally realized that scrapbooking would allow me to incorporate my love for both fabric and paper in my work.

My favorite crafting style is an 'antique-vintage' look. I enjoy tea-dying rickrack and ribbons and aging pages to look old. My scrapbook and journal pages remind me of small pieces of quilts and how much I love putting all the pieces together."

Materials:

Red Cardstock: Bazzil
Patterned Paper (Books): Design Originals
School Paper: Making Memories
Letters for "Child": 7gypsies
Alphabet Stickers: Pebbles, Inc. and Wordsworth
Alphabet Ransom Stickers: Rusty Pickle
Mini Tag: FoofaLa Industries
Large Tag: DMD Industries
Coffee and Sepia Archival Inkpads: Ranger Industries
Lamp Black Inkpad: Nick Bantok
Alphabet Rubber Stamps: Postmodern Design and PSX

FoofaBets Letters and Oval Cardstock Label Holder: FoofaLa
Label Type: Dymo
Bingo Piece ("u") and Wooden Alphabet Piece ("1"): Li'l Davis Designs
Decorative Brad: Making Memories
Adhesives: Hermafix; Scrappy Glue by Magic Scraps
Other: Photograph, fabric, embroidery floss, ribbons and antique tape measure
Tools: Mundial pinking shears, FoofaLa aging sponge and #10 embroidery needle

INSTRUCTIONS PAGE 66

A Swing pg 64

Instructions:

1. Using pinking shears, cut a piece of light colored chenille fabric.

2. Print black and white photo using computer and photo printer.

3. Mat photo onto red textured cardstock with one side trimmed using pinking shears.

4. Attach photo to fabric using a small dots of Scrappy Glue. Be sure to only use a small amount of this glue or picture will be lumpy.

5. Attach number stickers to bottom right corner of red mat indicating the year the photo was taken.

6. Attach a strip of schoolbook paper to the bottom of the page under fabric.

7. Attach a piece of quilted muslin to top right side of page.

8. Using embroidery floss, stitch through the front of quilted muslin and then back through the front. Tie a knot on the front of the page for decoration.

9. Using grade school paper as your background, spell out a quote of your choice. I used alphabet stamps, alphabet stickers, FoofaBets by FoofaLa, Dymo Tape and various three-dimensional pieces from Li'l Davis Designs to spell out my quote.

10. Handwrite person's name on top of the grade school paper.

11. Attach quote to the top of the quilted muslin.

12. Using FoofaLa aging sponges and a brown inkpad, age a large tag.

13. Complete the rest of your quote on tag and attach to schoolbook paper on bottom of the page.

14. Add a decorative brad in the hole on tag.

15. Tie several ribbons to a piece of antique tape measure and attach to bottom of photo using Scrappy Glue.

Tea Party
Invitation
Kim Henkel

Materials:

Floral Patterned Paper: SEI

Little Rabbit Patterned Paper: Anna Griffin

Dry Cleaning Ticket Patterned Paper: Mustard Moon

Crème Cardstock: Bazzil

Pink Mini File Folder: FoofaLa

Shabby Labels: FoofaLa

Tags and Mini Tags: FoofaLa

Coffee and Sepia Archival Inkpads: Ranger Industries

Lamp Black Pigment Ink: Nick Bantok

Rubber Stamps: "When" by Stampotique; "What" and "Where" by All Night Media/Plaid; Alphabet Rubber Stamps (all other words) by PSX; Single Heart by Paper Inspirations; Row of Hearts by Printworks

"Pixies" Little Baby Images: FoofaLa

FoofaBets Letters: FoofaLa

Fibers and Velvet Ribbon: FoofaLa

Paper Flower: Making Memories

Buttons, Rickrack and Ribbon: Local Craft or Fabric Store

Metal Clips: 7gypsies

Metal Silver Mini Frame: FoofaLa

Adhesives: Hermafix; Scrappy Glue by Magic Scraps

Other: White packing string

Tools: Mundial Pinking Shears and FoofaLa aging sponge

Instructions:

1. Using inkpads and FoofaLa aging sponge, age three large shipping tags, one small tag, and one mini file folder. The mini file folder will hold all the elements of the invitation and makes it easy for the recipient to view all tags.

2. Using two different FoofaLa Shabby Labels create the stripe and floral frame on the front of the file folder. Cut the middle of the Shabby Label out on both and then glue one set together to create the frame.

3. Use FoofaBets to create "Tea Party" on the mini file folder.

4. Add 7gypsies metal clips to keep the folder closed on both sides.

5. "Age" a paper flower using an inkpad and FoofaLa sponge.

6. Glue paper flower to file folder using Scrappy Glue.

7. Glue antique button to center of flower.

8. Tie a ribbon around the folder for additional detail.

9. Cut a teabag tag out of crème cardstock and punch a small hole in the top for packing string.

10. Stamp "It's a" on the teabag tag and adhere to the file folder.

11. For shipping tags, add all the details of your party using various patterned papers, cardstock, alphabet stamps, clip art or other embellishments of your choice.

12. Attach fibers and ribbons to the shipping tags.

13. Finish your invitation by placing all the tags in the folder.

"The inspiration for this fun invitation came from a love of tags ... how fun would it be to receive such a special invitation to a tea party? I thought a tea party should be very frilly and pink, which is why I chose to use FoofaLa Pixies." Kim

Materials (Book):

Cardstock: Bazzil

Artist's Canvas: Local Art Supply

Large "M" Postage: MegaBets by FoofaLa

Postage Alphabets: FoofaBets by FoofaLa

Blue Grotto Inkpad: Fresco

Orange VersaColor Pigment Inkpad: Tsukineko

Flower Rubber Stamp: Hero Arts

Ribbons, Red and Orange Netting and Black Pom Poms: Local Fabric Store

Beads and Large Yellow Rickrack: Local Antique Store

Embroidery Floss: DMC Industries

Bottle Cap: Li'l Davis Designs

Eyelets: Making Memories

Adhesive: Provo Craft Double-Sided Tape

Other: Two different pieces of 10" x 12" fabric

Tools: Mundial pinking shears, FoofaLa aging sponges, fabric scissors and sewing machine

Materials (Pages):

Cardstock: Bazzil and Memory Lane

Patterned Paper: KI Memories, Chatterbox, Doodlebug, SEI and K&Company

Mini File Folders: FoofaLa

Library Pocket Holder: Li'l Davis Designs

Tags: DMD Designs, America Tag and FoofaLa

Postage Alphabets: FoofaBets by FoofaLa

Cardstock Stickers: Real Life by Pebbles, Inc.

Three Dimensional Letter Stickers: K&Company

Alphabet Rub-Ons: Making Memories and Li'l Davis Designs

Alphabet Stickers: KI Memories and 7gypsies

Ransom Type Alphabet Stickers: Rusty Pickle

Wordfetti Stickers: Making Memories

Clock Sticker and Tag Hole Reinforcers: Nostalgiques by Rebecca Sower/EK Success

Ice Candy: KI Memories

Number Block (used on page numbers): FoofaLa

Sepia, Coffee and Russet Archival Inkpads: Ranger Industries

Lamp Black Inkpad: Nick Bantok

Black Ink Pen (Size .05): Zig by EK Success

Rubber Stamps: Alphabet by Postmodern Design, Stampotique, PSX and All Night Media/Plaid; "Lounge Chair" by Stampa Barbara; "Alarm Clock" by 100 Proof Press and Rubber Stamps of America; "Large Polka Dot" and Decorative Frame by Stampotique; "Small Polka Dot" by Hero Arts; "Large Clock" by Postmodern Designs; "Large Flower" by Stampington & Co. and Paper Inspirations; "Sun" by Making Memories; "Champagne Label" by Stampers Anonymous; "Star and Heart" by Paper Inspirations - stamps that were used throughout the entire journal - not all are shown.

Computer Fonts: www.twopeasinabucket.com

Ribbons & Rickrack: Local Fabric Store

Buttons and Large Yellow Rickrack: Local Antique Store

Netting and Burlap: Local Fabric Store

Printed Twill: 7gypsies

Red Wood Frame: Li'l Davis Designs

Decorative Brads: Making Memories

Black Paper Clip and Bamboo Clip: 7gypsies

Decorative Paper Clips: Nostalgiques by Rebecca Sower/EK Success

Bottle Caps, Small Bottle Cap Letters and Metal Stencil Letters: Li'l Davis Designs

Eyelets: Making Memories

Adhesives: Hermafix; Provo Craft Double-Sided Tape

Other: Brads, white packing string, large orange envelope, grade school practice paper and library card

Tools: Mundial pinking shears, FoofaLa aging sponges and Dymo Label Maker

Instructions (book):

1. Cut two pieces of fabric to desired size. Using a sewing machine, sew right sides together and leave a large opening on one side.

2. Turn right sides out and slide in two large pieces and one small piece (spine) of artist's canvas or chipboard inside.

3. For the side that has the opening, tuck the raw edges inside and hand stitch opening closed.

4. Next, hand stitch using embroidery floss on either side of the spine to separate it from the canvas. This will keep the canvas or chipboard in place and create the look of a book.

5. Cut a piece of netting the length and stitch on inside of the book along the spine. This is what you will use to attach your pages.

6. Once you have the netting sewn in place, you are ready to attach your pages.

7. For pages, use heavy cardstock slightly smaller than your book. Decorate as you wish.

8. Attach three eyelets on the top of each page. Be sure to place the eyelets in the same location for each page to make it easier to attach them to the spine of your book.

9. Run a piece of ribbon through all pages and slip under the netting that you sewed into the spine of your book. Tie ribbons into a bow.

10. Decorate the cover with embellishments of your choice.

MexicanJournal Kim Henkel

Materials:

Cardstock: Bazzil

Patterned Paper: Colors By Design, Rocky Mountain Scrapbook Co. and Penny Black

Paper Frame: Forget Me Knot

Tag: Quickutz

Black Pigment Pad (Inkpad) : Nick Bantok

Alphabet Stamps: Barnes & Noble and PSX

100% Cotton Osnaburg Fabric: P&B Textiles

Embroidery Floss: Flower Thread by DMC

Metal Frame: Making Memories

Frame Charm: Impress Rubberstamps or Local Craft Store

Tin Heart: Dizzy Frizzy

Adhesives: Hermafix; Scrappy Glue by Magic Scraps

Other: Photo, antique crocheted squares, antique wool strip and ribbon

Instructions:

1. Cut a large rectangle of patterned paper and attach to the top of cardstock.

2. Cut another piece of patterned paper and attach to the top of the previous patterned paper.

3. Cut a piece of patterned paper and attach to the bottom of the page.

4. Using a computer and photo quality printer, print photo in black and white and attach to top right side of page.

5. Using computer fonts and rubber stamps print journaling on small square of cardstock and attach to page.

6. Glue a strip of antique lace to bottom of patterned paper under photo.

7. Add a pre-made paper frame to photo.

8. Attach antique wool to bottom of page using small dots of Scrappy Glue.

9. Using black stamp ink and alphabet stamps, print "Mom" on a small piece of osnaburg fabric.

10. Using a needle and three strands of embroidery floss, primitively stitch lines above and below "Mom" on the osnaburg fabric.

11. Frame a small photo using a Making Memories metal frame.

12. Using computer fonts, print journaling on small tag and attach to metal frame with ribbon.

13. Add two photos to the small frame charms and attach to page.

14. Run a piece of ribbon through the two small frame charms, adding a metal heart finish by tying ribbon to paper frame.

The journaling says it all. I am so proud of my mom and wanted to do a page to share that with her and whoever browses through my scrapbook. I tied the photos of my brother and myself to the frame with ribbon and added a metal heart to represent us tied together with love.   Kim

Mom Kim Henkel
Scrapbook Page

I must have done something really special to have you as my MOM and for that matter you were my dad too! I always remember giving you Mother's Day and Father's Day cards! I admire all you did to instill such strong values in Gary and me! You always tell us how proud you are of us but today, I want to tell you how proud I am of YOU! Thank you MOM for all you did for us and continue to do!
February 2003 xoxo

One of Mom's favorite quilts I made!

MOM

Wilber & Gertrude
Scrapbook Page
Dawne Renee Pitts

I found this lovely picture in an antique store and was immediately drawn to this cute couple. He looks so mischievous, and she so prim and proper. I can just imagine that he's just popped the question, and she's so excited but trying to remain reserved. Dawne

Dawne Renee Pitts began scrapbooking four years ago. After her first trip to a scrapbook store, she was instantly hooked. Since that time, she has participated in various round robin journals, and is on the design team for FoofaLa. She also teaches classes for her local scrapbook store, Scrapbook Sensation in Alpine, California. Dawne loves to scrap everyday events, and to make handmade gifts for her friends. Her current addictions are rubber stamping (particularly alphabet stamps — she owns over 50 sets!), and brightly colored patterned papers.

Dawn writes: "*My hobby has quickly taken over my life, and I couldn't be happier! I love being in my tiny loft apartment, surrounded by my stamps, inks, papers, vintage buttons, and jars and jars of ribbon. When I'm not at my "real" job as a legal secretary, you can find me in my loft with the windows open, the candles burning, and either an eclectic mix of CDs spinning or one of my numerous favorite movies on the DVD player. I'm so honored to be included with this group of talented and inspiring artists.*"

Materials:

Desert Sun Paper: Bazzill

Patterned Paper: Anna Griffin, Chatterbox and 7gypsies

Playing Card: 7gypsies

Adhesive-Backed Words/Letters: Li'l Davis Designs and Rusty Pickle

FoofaBets, Mini File Folder and Tags: FoofaLa

Van Dyke Brown Dye Inkpad: Nick Bantok

Pumpkin Pie, Sugar Plum and Apple Cinnamon Vintage Ink: Ranger Industries

Black and Barn Red Memories Dye Ink Pad: Stewart Superior Corporation

Russet Archival Dye inkpad: Ranger Industries

Tim Holz Distress "Old Paper" Dye Inkpad: Ranger Industries

Rubber Stamps: "Front Page" Alphabet by Postmodern Design, Alphabets by Hero Arts and Brenda Walton for All Night Media/Plaid, "Dot Stamp" by Stampotique, "Heart Line" by Printworks and "Heart Pair" by Paper Inspirations

Decorative Brads: Making Memories

Paper Clip and Lace Ribbon: Rebecca Sower for EK Success

Light Blue Oval Label Holder: FoofaLa

Adhesives: Pioneer Photo Memory Mounting Tape

Other: Library card and antique buttons

Tools: FoofaLa aging sponge, sandpaper, corner rounder and pinking shears

I am a ribbon freak! I have huge jars full of ribbon, and every time I go to a new store, I buy at least two yards of everything yummy. I wanted the tag to just look like bits and pieces, to represent the view of my fun jars here in my studio.

D a w n e

Wilbur & Gertrude Scrapbook Page pg.72

Instructions:

1. Age Desert Sun cardstock with Nick Bantok Van Dyke Brown ink using FoofaLa aging sponge.

2. Sand edges of all patterned papers and attach to page; attach photo to page.

3. Trim beige cardstock into two tags, one larger than the other, and use corner rounder to round corners. Age both tags with Nick Bantok Van Dyke Brown Ink using FoofaLa aging sponge. On the larger tag, use the Dot stamp by Stampotique with the Tim Holtz Old Paper ink.

4. Use pinking shears to cut two small squares of the 7gypsies paper and attach to the larger tag; using the Nick Bantok Inks and Ranger Inks, ink edges of FoofaBets to color and age each letter.

5. Attach the "W" and the "G" to the larger tag and add the "&" FoofaBet; attach tag to page.

6. Using Nick Bantok Van Dyke Brown ink, age edges of the mini file folder and tape folder shut. Attach folder to page at a slight angle; attach the inked FoofaBet numbers to the tag top of the file folder.

7. Remove the inside oval tag from the Shabby Label and ink the edges of the frame. Attach to file folder. Adhere the 7gypsies playing card with a FoofaLa definition over it. Cut out various other FoofaLa definitions and stick them in the top edge of the mini file folder.

8. Age the index card with the Nick Bantok and Archival Russet inks. Computer-print journaling using "Love Letter" computer font downloaded from the internet. Using the Memories Barn Red ink, stamp the "Heart Line" and "Heart Pair" stamps onto the index card. Insert the index inside the file folder at an angle. Hold the index card in place with the paper clip by Rebecca Sower, along with some tape under the top of the index card.

9. Using the Tim Holtz Distress Ink in Old Paper, stamp a polka dot onto the light blue FoofaLa oval label holder and ink the edges with Van Dyke Brown ink.

10. Stamp "Beginning" onto the smaller oval corner tag using the Memories Black ink and the Brenda Walton alpha stamps. Using the Memories Barn Red ink, stamp with Hero Arts alpha stamps. Spell the word "life" with a mixture of the Li'l Davis Designs and Rusty Pickle letter stamps. Attach oval corner tag to page and antique button to tag.

11. On the light blue oval labelholder, stamp "gether" using the Front Page alphabet by Postmodern Design. Adhere an aged and inked "2" FoofaBet. String ribbon through the end of the label holder and attach tag to page with decorative brad.

12. Cut a small strip of the antique lace and attach is across the top right corner of the photo using the decorative brads.

Materials:

Patterned Paper: SEI

Orange Paper and Green Cardstock: Local Craft Store

Mini File Folio: FoofaLa

"Family Expressions" Wordfetti Stickers: Making Memories

Other Stickers: Real Life by Pebbles, Inc.; Li'l Davis Designs; Rusty Pickle

Tags to Go: FoofaLa

Black Memories Dye Inkpad: Stewart Superior Corporation

Chinese Red Inkpad: Antiquities

Tim Holz "Old Paper" Distress Inkpad: Ranger Industries

VanDyke Brown Inkpad: Nick Bantock

Rubber Stamps: Border by Just for Fun; "Dream Fly Jubilate" by Rubbermoon; Small Star by Our Lady of Rubber; "Swirl" and "Come & Play" by Claudia Rose; "Heart Line" by Printworks; Finger and Alphabet Stamps by Brenda Walton; "Dots" background by Stampotique; Gothic Lower Case Alphabet Stamps by Postmodern Design

Playfuls Pixies: FoofaLa

Silver Tassie: FoofaLa

Other: Various ribbons and vintage photo

Tools: Pinking shears and hole punch

Instructions:

1. Age the mini file folio with Van Dyke Brown ink.

2. Cut a small portion of the SEI paper and pink one edge; age with Van Dyke Brown ink.

3. Attach the picture at an angle.

4. Stamp the Dream Fly Jubilate stamp on orange paper and cut out and adhere across the bottom of the picture.

5. Stamp border on green cardstock; cut out with pinking shears. Stamp "Come & Play" inside the border. Using Chinese Red ink, stamp small stars inside border and adhere to page.

6. Punch three holes down both sides of the file folio and tie ribbons in each hole.

7. Age a FoofaLa Tag to Go with Van Dyke Brown ink.

8. Cut out the FoofaLa Pixie and pink the top edge. Age with Van Dyke Brown ink

9. Using various letter stamps, spell out "Girlfriends" along the edge of the Pixie.

10. Stamp "Crop" using the Postmodern Design alpha stamps.

11. Using Chinese Red ink, stamp the Heart Line stamp across the top of tag.

12. Tie on small piece of black and white gingham.

Invitation to Girlfriends Crop
Dawne Renee Pitts

Come & Play

ream fly Jubilate Imagine create

girlfriends crop

ARTSY

CRAYOLA

We have such a fun time when my best friend Kim, her mom Sue and I get together to shop, crop or just hang out. I wanted to invite them to my house for a fun girlfriends crop. I found this vintage photo of three friends in an antique shop and knew it was perfect for the invitation! Dawne

Give Me the Simple Life

Dawne Renee Pitts

Materials:

Cardstock: Bazzill

Vintage ABC Collage Paper:
Beth Cote for Design Originals

Old Tag Letters: Nostalgiques
by Rebecca Sower/EK Success

Letter Disc and Frame:
Li'l Davis Designs

Tags: FoofaLa

Van Dyke Brown Inkpad:
Nick Bantok

Pumpkin Pie Vintage Inkpad:
Ranger Industries

Black Dye Inkpad:
Stuart Superior Corporation

**Antique Alphabet Rubber
Stamps:** PSX

**"Hodge Podge" and "Quirky"
Large Alphabet Rubber Stamps:**
Postmodern Design

FoofaBets Letters: FoofaLa

Wooden Game Piece Alphas:
Li'l Davis Designs

Index Plates and Paper Clip:
7gypsies

Other: Embroidery floss, vintage
rickrack and fabric

Tools: Pinking shears, sewing
machine and FoofaLa aging
sponge

Instructions:

1. Sew piece of fabric to the Bazzill
   cardstock.

2. Thread the embroidery thread
   through the holes in the
   7gypsies index plates and
   squeeze the plates to the sides
   of the photo.

3. Attach photo to the fabric mat at
   an angle.

4. Cut out the "S" from the Beth
   Cote paper and pink the edges;
   then age with Nick Bantok Van
   Dyke Brown ink and FoofaLa
   aging sponge.

5. Age the edges of the FoofaLa
   tags. Using the mixture of alpha
   stickers, stamps and FoofaBets,
   attach your journaling to the
   tags.

"This picture was taken at a small
candy/antique store close to my house.
It's just on the side of the road, with an
old train and circus car out front.
When you go in the door of the store,
you're greeted by jars of penny candies,
sodas, and antiques. Definitely a step
back to a *simpler time.* It's one of my
absolute favorite places in the world!" Dawne

Mr. Pitts
Dawne Renee Pitts

Scrapbook Page

Materials:

Cardstock: Bazzill

Basic Grey Paper: Alaskan Blue

Other Papers: KI Memories, Chatterbox and Paperfever

Alpha Fetti Stickers: Making Memories

Dome Stickers: Marcella by Kay

Inverted Roman Alpha Sticker: Wordsworth

Bubble Letters: KI Memories

Rub-Ons: Scrapworks

Graffiti: Art Warehouse

Vintage Labels: Li'l Davis Designs

Run On Transfers: Brenda Walton for K&Company

Tags: KI Memories

Black Dye Inkpad: Memories

Van Dyke Brown Dye Inkpad: Nick Bantok

Chinese Red Pigment Inkpad: Antiquities Ink

Rubber Stamps: Breite Italienne Alpha Stamps by Chronicle Books, Small Heart by Hero Arts and Olive Dog by Claudia Rose

Adhesive: Pioneer Double-Sided Photo Tape

Other: Photograph

Instructions:

Adhere photo to cardstock and embellish with various scraps of paper, journaling and stamps, as shown.

"*My dearest dog Wally passed away from cancer in March 2004. This is one of the first layouts I've been able to do about him since his death. Rather than do a serious layout, I wanted to just do sort of a random layout of some of his silly nicknames, using bright colors and fun stamps. I have so many* **wonderful memories** *of Mr. Pitts, and I wanted to get some of them down on paper to begin the healing process.*" Dawne

XO XO XO

Dearest Kim

I have always loved this picture of you, taken in the backyard at Grandma and Grandpa's house ... fine. You loved

watering GRANDMA'S GARDEN

1976

grow (gro), *v.t.* [grew, *p.p.* grown, *p.pr.* growing], to cultivate; *v.i.* to increase in stature or size by natural organic development; be produced by vegetation; increase; flourish; thrive; become; advance; become fixed or attached. *Syn.* vegetate, expand.

belle (bel), *n.* a young and beautiful lady; a reigning beauty.

cu-ri-ous (rius), *adj.* desirous to see or know something strange; inquisitive; scrutinizing; exact; extraordinary.

life (lif), *n.* animate vitality; union of soul and ... period between birth and death ... *Syn.* animation, vivacity.

Scrapbook Page
Watering Grandma's Garden
Dawne Renee Pitts

Materials:

Leapfrog and Pinecone Cardstock: Bazzill

Cosmopolitan Collection Patterned Papers: Making Memories

Pink Cardstock: Local Craft Store

Adhesive-Backed Words/Letters: Real Life by Pebbles, Inc., Li'l Davis Designs and Rusty Pickle

Simply Stated Rub-On Alphabet (Heidi): Making Memories

FoofaBets, FanciBets and Definitions: FoofaLa

Blue Key Tag: Local Office Supply

Van Dyke Brown and Rose Madder Dye Inkpads: Nick Bantok

Pumpkin Pie Vintage Ink: Ranger Industries

Chinese Red Pigment Inkpad: Antiquities

Moon Garden Rubber Stamp: Jill Penney for Stampotique

Alphabet Stamps: PSX and Hero Arts

Pink Snaps: Making Memories

Paper Clip: 7gypsies

Adhesives: Pioneer Photo Tape

Other: Blue string envelope, vintage ribbons, rickrack, buttons and silk flowers

Tools: Pinking shears and FoofaLa aging sponge

Instructions:

1. Cut the Making Memories papers in various sizes and shapes and attach to Leapfrog cardstock.

2. Print photo onto canvas art paper and mat on Pinecone cardstock at an angle. Attach to page and secure with pink snaps. Using rub-ons for the date.

3. Ink the edges of the blue string envelope with Nick Bantok inks and stamp the Moon Garden image with the Chinese Red ink.

4. Spell out the word "Watering" using a mixture of all letter stickers.

5. Stamp the word "Grandma's" with Chinese Red ink.

6. Age and ink a mixture of FoofaBets and FanciBets to spell out the word "garden" and attach to the envelope. Adhere the envelope to the page at an angle.

7. Attach ribbons and rickrack to the top of the envelope.

8. Cut out a tall journaling block of pink cardstock and use pinking shears to pink the top. Age the block with Nick Bantok Van Dyke Brown ink. Stamp "XOXOXOXO" across top using Hero Arts stamps. Insert into envelope and hold in place with the 7gypsies paper clip.

9. String brown gingham ribbon through the blue plastic key tag and attach to page; adhere a FoofaBet to the key tag.

10. Cut out several inked and aged FoofaLa definitions and mount to the Pinecone cardstock; cut at various sizes and angles and adhere to page at various angles. Attach pink snaps to corner.

This is a picture of my best friend Kim Henkel in her grandma's garden when she was a little girl. I wanted to do a layout that was fun and very pink to honor my sweet friend. I printed the picture onto canvas art paper to give it some texture, and asked Kim's mom, Sue, to do the journaling for me. I included "XOXOXOXO" (hugs & kisses) across the top of the journaling tag because that is how Kim, Sue & I always sign our emails to each other. Dawne

Invite someone dangerous to Tea

sark

Invite
Someone Dangerous
to Tea · Dawne Renee Pitts
Scrapbook Page

Materials:

Sweetheart Cardstock: Bazzill

Hippy Chick Patterned Paper: SEI

Other Papers: KI Memories

Bubble Letters: KI Memories

Label: Melissa Frances

Rub-Ons by Heidi Font: Making Memories

Other Rub-Ons: Scrapworks, FanciBet by FoofaLa

Chipboard Alphabet: Li'l Davis Designs

Black Dye Inkpad: Memories

Van Dyke Brown Inkpad: Nick Bantock

Playful Alphabet Stamps: Hero Arts

Colored Buttons: SEI

Metal Bookplate: Making Memories

Adhesives: Glue Stick

Other: Vintage buttons, ribbon, children's writing tablet paper, piece of tea-dyed muslin and iron-on transfer

Tools: Pinking shears

Instructions:

1. Print photo onto iron-on transfer, and iron onto tea-dyed muslin. Cut out photo and fray edges of the muslin by pulling threads out on the sides.

2. Cut out a strip of the SEI Hippy Chick paper, pink one end. Attach the Melissa Frances label, and tie various ribbons around the strip of paper. Apply to the left side of the cardstock.

3. Cut out journaling block from the children's writing table paper, pink the edges of one end and age with Van Dyke Brown ink. Using a mixture of letter stickers, rub-ons and chipboard alphas, attach title.

4. Cut a small piece of KI Memories paper and stamp the author of the quote (SARK) on it, using the alphabet stamp set. Attach the small piece of KI paper to the bottom right hand of the cardstock. Tie a piece of ribbon around the right edge of the bookplate and attach over the work with brads.

5. Lightly adhere the photo square to the page. Using a mixture of vintage buttons and the SEI colored buttons, frame the picture. Run a piece of ribbon through a large antique button and attach it to the top left-hand corner of the photo square.

I used to think that vintage photos were always stiff and serious. However, the more I snoop around antique stores, the more I find photos full of character and fun. This was one such photo. These three ladies looked like such good friends, and were dressed up for some special occasion ... perhaps a ladies tea. I love to combine vintage photos with bright, unexpected colors and wanted to use a fun quote to go with this photo. One of my favorite authors is SARK, and this quote just seemed perfect! Dawne

WHEN YOUR'e in over your HEAD

AUG · 65

SWIM with your HEART

ing-swimming-singing Aqu
B O lor
whole family

Swim with Your Heart
Scrapbook Page

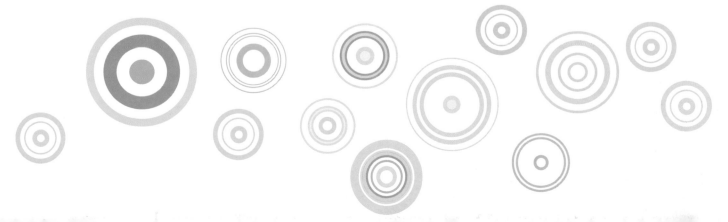

Dawne Renee Pitts

Materials:

Pink Cardstock: Bazzill

Weathered Cardstock: Paper Loft

Poolside Runway Paper: KI Memories

Pastel Ring-A-Ding Paper: Paper Fever

Snow/Winter Block Paper: My Mind's Eye

Heidi Mini Rub-Ons: Making Memories

FoofaBets and Tags: FoofaLa

Van Dyke Brown and Charcoal Grey Dye Inkpads:
Nick Bantok

Pumpkin Pie Vintage Ink: Ranger Industries

Chinese Red Pigment Inkpad: Antiquities

Rubber Stamps: Brenda Walton for All Night Media,
"Heart Line" by Print Works and "Classic lower case"
by Hero Arts

Light Blue Artist Playing Card: FoofaLa

Wooden Letters: Li'l Davis Designs

Colored Brads: Making Memories

Other: Purple felt and various brightly colored ribbons

Tools: Pinking shears

Instructions:

1. Begin with the pink cardstock base and add small rectangle of the Paper Loft cardstock to the lower left corner.

2. Cut a piece of the My Mind's Eye Snow/Winter block paper and attach it to the right edge of the pink cardstock.

3. Cut two long strips of the KI Memories and Paper Fever paper and pink the right edges. Attach to paper at angles to each other.

4. Cut a mat of the purple felt and pink the edges. Attach to page at an angle. Attach photo to the felt. Attach colored brads and ribbons to the right side of the photo.

5. Age the FoofaLa tags with the Nick Bantok and Ranger Inks and attach a mixture of alphabet stamps, FoofaBets and Li'l Davis words to do your journaling.

"This is a photo of me at age three. I was deathly afraid of the pool, but insisted on going each time my two older brothers went. I spent most of my days at the baby pool, clutching my little yellow and blue lifesaver. I love the fact that my hair is all done, so that I looked nice at the pool!   Dawne

AmyWellenstein

Happily Every After

"The photo used in this project is one taken of me on my wedding day. It was shortly after our ceremony and I was crowded around with family and friends, laughing uncontrollably from sheer joy. It was truly the happiest day of my life. The embellishments I used signify that my husband was the key to me finding happiness ... ever after." Amy

Amy Wellenstein maintains a full time technical career by day but immerses herself in creating art at night and on weekends. She designs rubber stamps for Stampotique Originals in Phoenix, Arizona and has taught classes in paper arts for the last four years. In 2003, she was invited to teach at several stores in New England. Her work has been featured in *Somerset Studios, Return to Asia, Rubber Stamper,* and *Stamper's Sampler.*

Amy writes: "I live in Peoria, Arizona with my husband George and our two short fuzzy children; Twitch, our antisocial tiger cat and Bleu, our blue-eyed Dalmatian. Once married, I moved and graduated from creating art on the kitchen table to having my very own studio. It was a spare bedroom with lots of closet space for supplies and big windows that let in wonderful natural light. Sometimes I get so caught up in my art, I don't even come out of my studio to eat.

If I were asked what inspires me, I,d have to say color and texture. I tend to create things that are very balanced, but color and texture always prevail. I also love collecting bits and pieces of 'stuff', wherever I am. Some of my most treasured finds have been on the side of the road on bike rides and along the shore at the beach.

I became involved in paper arts on a business trip to Colorado. After the seminar and dinner, I found a small rubber stamp store around the corner. Although I had never stamped before, I wandered in and ended up spending several hundred dollars and the rest is history. Once back home in Arizona, I did a little research to see if there were any stamp stores near me. To my delight, I discovered Stampotique Originals. I never imagined that my new hobby would develop into something that provides me with such pleasure today and has introduced me to so many wonderful people.

I have dabbled in many areas such as polymer clay, rubberstamping, altered books and soldering. I recently tried to figure out exactly what my 'thing' is and finally decided it's whatever's new! At the moment, it is any- thing with vintage family photos. I love bring- ing new life to old photos, especially of rela- tives who are no longer with us. I call them 'rescued relatives.'

My art is ever evolving. I have found that in creating art, I've created myself."

Pink Photo Clipboard pg 84

Materials:

Ledger Printed Paper: K&Company

Embossed Sticker: Brianna Postage Stamps by K&Company

Acrylic Glazing Liquid: Golden Artist Colors, Inc.

Quinacridone Magenta Fluid Acrylic: Golden Artist Colors, Inc.

Acrylic Gesso: Liquitex

Medium Magenta and Parchment Acrylic Paint: Liquitex

Coffee and Carnation Archival Inkpads: Ranger Industries

Onyx Black VersaFine Inkpad: Tsukineko

Rubber Stamps: "Antique Border" by Stampotique Originals; Brenda Walton Alphabet Set by All Night Media/Plaid; Script Background by A Stamp in the Hand

Ribbon: Local Craft Store

Metal Messages, Keyhole and Key: Metal Memorabilia by Li'l Davis Designs

Adhesives: Xyron Machine; The Ultimate! Glue

Other: Clipboard, photograph and sandpaper

Instructions: (both clipboards are the same)

1. Lightly sand the clipboard, then coat with a layer of gesso; let dry.

2. Use glazing medium and various acrylic paints to color the surface of the clipboard; let dry.

3. Stamp images and phrases with rubber stamps.

4. Use Xyron machine to adhere photographs to the painted surface.

5. Embellish with patterned papers, stickers, metal findings, ribbon, etc. (Note: Paint antique metal findings with cream colored acrylic paint for an aged look.)

Aqua Photo Clipboard pg 84

Materials:

Script and Buttons Paper: K&Company

Acrylic Glazing Liquid: Golden Artist Colors, Inc.

Phthalo Green Fluid Acrylic: Golden Artist Colors, Inc.

Acrylic Gesso: Liquitex

Parchment and Light Blue Acrylic Paint: Liquitex

Coffee and Aqua Archival Inkpads: Ranger Industries

Onyx Black VersaFine Inkpad: Tsukineko

Rubber Stamps: "Numbers," "Large Love Definition," "Torn," and "Measuring Tape" by Stampotique Originals

Metal Messages: Metal Memorabilia by Li'l Davis Designs

Adhesives: Xyron Machine; The Ultimate! Glue

Other: Clipboard, photograph and sandpaper

Paper Doll Tag Book
Amy Wellenstein

Materials:

Button Printed Paper and 1795 Gazette Paper: Life's Journey by K&Company

Green Patterned Damask Embossed Paper and Butterfly Collage Paper: K&Company

Designer Silver Script: Die Cuts with a View

Dark Gray Paper: Mi Teintes by Canson

Duffel Bag Paper: Everafter Scrapbook Company

Colette Paper: Laura Ashley by EK Success

Brown Floral, Antique Letters and Black Antique Dots Papers: Daisy D's

English Floral Frames and Tags: Grand Adhesions by K&Company (cover)

Itty Bitty Love Cardstock Stickers: Real Life by Pebbles, Inc.

Definitions: FoofaLa

Large Tags: Local Office Supply or Local Craft Store

Titanium White Acrylic Paint: Liquitex

Magnolia Bud VersaMagic Inkpad: Tsukineko

Black Onyx VersaFine Inkpad: Tsukineko

Rubber Stamps: Brenda Walton Alphabet Set Rubber Stamp by All Night Media/Plaid; "Antique Border" by Stampotique Originals

Ruban Ribbon (1/4"): 7gypsies

Small Safety Pins: Darice

Penny and Nickel Bobs: FoofaLa

Adhesives: UHU Glue Stick; Scotch Double-Stick Tape

Other: Mat board (for cover), color copies of vintage photos and pencil

Tools: Sewing machine

Instructions:

1. Topstitch along one edge of a long piece of dark gray paper.

2. Fold the bottom of the strip up to form a pocket; stitch along ends to secure pocket.

3. Cut out several vintage photos of women and children, trimming the images off at the waist.

4. Use patterned paper to create "skirts" for each person; glue the images and the skirts to the tags.

5. Outline each image with white acrylic paint and random pencil lines; stamp phrases along the pencil lines and numbers at the top of each tag.

6. Use small safety pins to attach a small "bob" to the top of each tag through the hole.

7. Adhere definitions to each pocket.

8. Stamp antique border along the bottom of the tag book using Magnolia Bud ink; use the same ink and an alphabet set to stamp "PAPER DOLLS" across the top repeatedly (under tags).

9. Adhere duffel bag patterned paper to two pieces of mat board for the front and back covers; use double-stick tape to assemble the book.

10. Adhere sticker frames to the front cover; embellish with vintage photos and rubber stamps.

11. Tie the book closed with a piece of silk ribbon.

Altered Box of Cards

Amy Wellenstein

"*This project was a celebration of* shape *and* color. *The photos feature members of my family as well as some 'rescued relatives.' This was a great opportunity to experiment with several techniques and embellishments in the same project. A full house has never been so much* fun." Amy

Materials:

State of Louisiana Paper; Brianna Ledger & Script Paper; Folded Wood Tape Measure Paper; Ledger Printed Paper and Script & Buttons Paper: K&Company

Black Script Paper (Sommes): 7gypsies

Watercolor Paper (140 lb. Stock): Strathmore

Small FoofaBets Paper: FoofaLa

Ruler: Nostalgiques by Rebecca Sower/EK Success

Button Frame: Grand Adhesions/Life's Journey by K&Company

Page Pebble: Making Memories

Gingham Ribbon and Button Border: Marcella by Kay

Brass Alphabet: Life's Journey Metal Art by K&Company

Small Alphabet Charms: Making Memories

Bubble Type (Script Black with White Font) and Bubble Phrases: Li'l Davis Designs

Dictionary Thoughts Cardstock Sticker: Real Life by Pebbles, Inc.

Acrylic Glazing Liquid: Golden Artist Colors, Inc.

Fluid Acrylic (Green Gold, Hansa Yellow Medium, Transparent Red Iron Oxide, Permanent Violet Dark, Quinacridone Magenta, Iridescent Copper Light, Dioxazine Purple, Phthalo Green): Golden Artist Colors

Acrylic Gesso: Liquitex

Acrylic Paint (Light Violet, Medium Magenta, Brilliant Orange, Naphthol Crimson, Light Blue): Liquitex

Lumiere Paint (Halo,Violet, Gold): Jacquard Products

Archival Inkpad (Coffee, Sepia, Carnation, Maroon): Ranger Industries

Jet Black StazOn Inkpad: Tsukineko

Onyx Black VersaFine Inkpad: Tsukineko

Henna Prismacolor Pencil: Sanford

Rubber Stamps: "Alpha," "Numeric," "Alphabitties" alphabet set, "Joy Definition," "Spiraling out of Control," "Carol's Half," "Angel," "Word Collage," "Precious," "Antique Border" and "Lace Background" by Stampotique Originals; Brenda Walton Alphabet Set by All Night Media/Plaid; Script Background by A Stamp in the Hand; Stitched border by Stampers Anonymous; "Handprint" Alphabet Set by Turtle Press

Long Bar: 7gypsies

Brads and Snaps: Making Memories

Oval and Round Frames: Metal Memorabilia by Li'l Davis Designs

Brass Card Holder: Local Craft Store

Adhesives: Xyron Machine; UHU Glue Stick; Scotch Double-Stick Tape and Foam Tape; Mod Podge by Plaid

Other: Aluminum tape, mat board and paper ephemera

Tools: Fan brush, ball stylus, eyelet setter, hammer and hole punch

Instructions:

1. Use glazing medium, acrylic paints, and gesso to color several pieces of paper (old book pages, patterned scrap-book paper, sheet music, etc.). These pieces will be used to cover the house-shaped cards and the framed piece on the lid.

2. Construct a house-shaped box and lid from mat board.

3. Use Mod Podge by Plaid to cover the box and lid with patterned paper.

4. Use a fan brush to apply a light coat of gesso on the outside of the box and lid (the gesso will soften the colors).

5. Cut a rectangular piece of mat board to fit on the cover; cover with aluminum tape and use a stylus to engrave a pattern around the edges. Antique with StazOn ink.

6. Cut a slightly smaller piece of mat board and cover it with one of the pages prepared in step 1.

7. Add a photograph, snaps, and various collage elements to this layer then use foam tape to attach it to the mat board piece prepared in step 5; adhere both layers to the lid of the box.

8. Adhere computer-generated words to the back of a rectangular page pebble. Line the page pebble with a scrap of aluminum tape and adhere it to the lid of the box.

9. Cut house-shaped cards from the watercolor paper. NOTE: The pages should be just slightly smaller than the base of the box.

10. Use glue stick to adhere the remaining papers from step 1 to the house-shaped cards (trim off excess).

11. Use photographs, stickers, rubber stamps, metal findings and various collage elements to decorate the cards; use adhesive backed letters or alphabet stamps to personalize your cards.

Materials:

"Fenetre" Journal: 7gypsies

Brown Travel Paper: Daisy D's

Script Borders Embossed Stickers (Ruler): Marcella by Kay

Travel Log Embossed Sticker: Black Label Words and Sayings by K&Company

Onyx Black VersaFine Inkpad: Tsukineko

Rubber Stamps: Italian Text by Rubber Baby Buggy Bumpers; Cancellation Marks from Tin Can Mail by Stampa Rosa

Mica: USArtQuest

Brads: Making Memories

Adhesive: UHU Glue Stick

Other: Old postage stamps and photograph

Instructions:

1. Adhere patterned paper to front cover.

2. Embellish with old postage stamps, rubber stamps, an old photo and stickers.

3. Secure a piece of mica over the window using brads.

" The Travel Journal is a collection of memoirs from a fictitious trip. I loved using the transparencies to give an illusion of depth. The photo on the front cover is from an old family photo album. A small piece of mica, held on with brads, framed the photo nicely. Amy "

(Cover)
Travel Journal Amy Wellenstein

Travel Journal Amy Wellenstein

Materials:

"Fenetre" Journal: 7gypsies

London Map Printed Vellum:
Life's Journey by K&Company

Brianna Ledger and Script Paper: K&Company

Travel Definition: Travel Phrase Stickers by Colorbok

Travel Documents and Paris Transparencies: 7gypsies

Dream Compass Printed Acetate: Life's Journey
by K&Company

Coffee Archival Inkpad: Ranger Industries

Onyx Black VersaFine Inkpad: Tsukineko

Brenda Walton Alphabet Set Rubber Stamps:
All Night Media/Plaid

Adhesives: UHU Glue Stick; Scotch Double-Stick Tape

Other: Vintage glassine envelope and photographs

Tools: Exacto Knife

Instructions:

LEFT PAGE:

1. Adhere paper to inside cover.

2. Attach glassine envelope using double stick tape.

3. Tuck photos and vellum map into envelope.

4. Adhere "souvenir" sticker next to envelope.

RIGHT PAGE:

1. Cut a window through two pages of the journal.

2. Use double-stick tape to secure a transparency between
the pages.

3. Stamp text around the window using an alphabet set.

4. Sponge dye-based ink (coffee) along the edges of the page.

5. Sew a small transparency to the outside edge of the page.

Travel Journal

Amy Wellenstein

Materials:

"Fenetre" Journal: 7gypsies

Postcard Printed Paper, London Map Printed Paper, Train Tickets Paper and Layered Documents Paper: Life's Journey by K&Company

Brown Travel Paper: Daisy D's

Magnetique: 7gypsies

Black Bubble Type: Li'l Davis Designs

Travel Documents and Paris Transparencies: 7gypsies

Onyx Black VersaFine Inkpad: Tsukineko

Fuzzy Alphabet Rubber Stamp (Large): Postmodern Design

Steel Ends and Silver Clips: 7gypsies

Dog Tag: A Lost Art

Ball Chain: Darice

Brads: Making Memories

Adhesives: Xyron Machine; UHU Glue Stick; Scotch Double-Stick Tape

Other: Walnut-stained envelope, key and round tag

Tools: Long-armed stapler

Instructions:

LEFT PAGE:

1. Layer several patterned papers on page.

2. Stamp "JOURNEY" along the top of page.

3. Attach a small transparency.

4. Use a steel end and brad to attach various metal findings.

RIGHT PAGE:

1. Fold patterned paper around the bottom and back of page.

2. Staple in place to form a pocket.

3. Spell out "Travel Documents" using bubble type.

4. Tuck various transparencies, maps and travel documents in the envelope.

Materials:

"Fenetre" Journal: 7gypsies

Train Tickets Paper: Life's Journey by K&Company

Red Floral Paper: The Paper Company

Black File Folio: FoofaLa

Adhesive-Backed Domed Alphabet: Life's Journey by K&Company

Coffee Archival Inkpad: Ranger Industries

Cloud White VersaMagic Inkpad: Tsukineko

Rubber Stamps: Cancellation Mark by Art Impressions; Egypt Poste by Stampa Rosa

Letterpress Twill: 7gypsies

Gold Photo Turns: 7gypsies

Brads: Making Memories

Adhesives: UHU Glue Stick; Scotch Double-Stick Tape; ProArt Black Photographic Tape

Other: Photographs and clear packing tape for photo transfer

Tools: Long-armed stapler

Instructions:

LEFT PAGE:

1. Use double-stick tape to adhere a black file folder to the page; tuck vintage documents inside the folder.
2. Use brads to attach gold photo turns on either side of the folder.
3. Stamp folder with cancellation marks using white ink.
4. Attach a packing tape transfer to the front of the folder using a long armed stapler.
5. Use bubble type to spell out "Memoirs" on the tab of the folder.
6. Age the edges of the page with dye-based ink.

RIGHT PAGE:

1. Crumple red floral paper and age with dye-based inks; adhere to page.
2. Use black photographic tape to hold the photo in place.
3. Use brads to adhere twill tape to the bottom of the page.

Travel Journal Amy Wellenstein

Come In To Play Journal

Amy Wellenstein

Materials:

"Maison" Gated Journal: 7gypsies

Antique Finish Paper: Daisy D's

Antique Ruler Sticker: Nostalgiques by Rebecca Sower/EK Success

License Plate Alphabet Stickers: The Paper Loft

Adhesive: UHU Glue Stick

Instructions:

1. Use glue stick to adhere brown patterned paper to both sides of the cover.

2. Use alphabet stickers to spell out "COME IN AND PLAY" on the cover.

3. Adhere an antique ruler sticker across the bottom of the cover.

Come In To Play Journal

Mariposa
Amy Wellenstein

Materials:

"Maison" Gated Journal: 7gypsies

Yellow Stripe Paper: Life's Journey by K&Company

Brianna Ledger and Script Paper: K&Company

Antique Rulers: Limited Edition

Black Label Words and Sayings Embossed Stickers: Life's Journey by K&Company

Monogram Letter Stickers: HyKo Products, Inc.

Coffee Archival Inkpad: Ranger Industries

Onyx Black VersaFine Inkpad: Tsukineko

Rubber Stamps: "Antique Border" by Stampotique Originals; Brenda Walton Alphabet Set by All Night Media/Plaid

Adhesives: Xyron Machine; UHU Glue Stick

Other: Paper ephemera and photograph

Instructions:

1. Stamp antique border along top of page using dye-based ink.

2. Adhere striped paper to the inside of the covers; embellish with black label tape stickers.

3. Construct a mini-collage using vintage photos, patterned paper, stickers and paper ephemera. Antique edges with dye-based ink, then mount to page using Xyron.

4. Use alphabet stamps to stamp title.

Come In To Play Journal

No Wings to Fly Amy Wellenstein

Materials:

"Maison" Gated Journal: 7gypsies

Number 9 Paper: Daisy D's

Script Printed Paper and Ledger Printed Paper:
Life's Journey by K&Company

Words on Paper Strips Embossed Stickers: Life's Journey
by K&Company

Sepia and Coffe Archival Inkpads: Ranger Industries

Onyx Black VersaFine Inkpad: Tsukineko

Walnut Ink: Paper & Ink

Rubber Stamps: "Antique Border" by Stampotique Originals;
Fuzzy Alphabet (Large) by Postmodern Design

Vine Stencil: American Traditional Stencils

"Wish" Charm: Marcella by Kay

Safety Pin: Dritz

Modeling Paste: Liquitex

Adhesives: Xyron Machine; The Ultimate! Glue

Other: Vintage buckle, twill tape, photograph and small
typewriter alphabet set

Tools: Palette knife

Instructions:

1. Adhere patterned paper to center page; antique top half with sepia dye-based ink.

2. Adhere and embellish photograph on center page.

3. Hang "Wish" charm from a vintage buckle using twill tape and safcty pin; glue to page.

4. Cut script patterned paper to the size of the left and right pages; run the pages through Xyron Machine but DO NOT remove the backing yet.

5. Use a palette knife to apply modeling paste; let dry.

6. Lay a stencil on the prepared papers and apply more modeling paste using the palette knife. Carefully remove stencil without smearing the wet paste; let dry.

7. Soak the two prepared pages in a tub of walnut ink to age.

8. Once dry, remove the Xyron backing and adhere the papers to the left and right pages; stamp phrases using black and brown inks.

Pixie
Come In To Play Journal
Amy Wellenstein

Materials:

"Maison" Gated Journal: 7gypsies

Concrete Paper: Facades by Far and Away

Ledger Printed Paper and Folded Wood Tape Measures Paper: Life's Journey by K&Company

Butterfly Collage, Brianna Ledger and Script Paper: K&Company

Rub On Alphabet: Alphawear Rub-Ons by Creative Imaginations

Words on Paper Strips Embossed Stickers: Life's Journey by K&Company

"XOXO" Tag: Real Life Cardstock Stickers by Pebbles, Inc.

"Memories" Bubble Phrase: Li'l Davis Designs

Sepia Archival Inkpad: Ranger Industries

Oval Frame: Metal Memorabilia by Li'l Davis Designs

Adhesives: Xyron Machine; UHU Glue Stick

Other: Vintage glassine envelopes and photograph

Tools: Sewing machine

Instructions:

1. Cover all three pages with butterfly collage paper.

2. Construct a mini-collage using vintage photos, cardstock stickers and patterned paper.

3. Antique edges with dye-based ink, then mount to the center page.

4. Mount "Memories" bubble word on oval frame and adhere above collage.

5. Sew glassine envelopes on left and right pages; insert script paper into envelopes and embellish with antiqued sticker words.

Come In To Play Journal
Sadie Mae Amy Wellenstein

Materials:

"Maison" Gated Journal: 7gypsies

Belle Jardiniere Paper: Daisy D's

Cream and Red Floral Paper: Anna Griffin

Khaki Duffel Bag Paper: Everafter Scrapbook Company

Red Cardstock: Bazzill

Sepia Archival Inkpad: Ranger Industries

"Dream" Charm: Marcella by Kay

Adhesives: Xyron Machine; UHU Glue Stick; Scotch Double-Stick Tape

Other: Vintage glassine envelopes, photograph and paper ephemera

Instructions:

1. Cover all three pages with red floral paper.
2. Construct a mini-collage using vintage photos, paper ephemera and a metal charm.
3. Antique edges with dye based ink. Layer on khaki patterned paper, then mount to center page.
4. Adhere glassine envelopes to left and right pages. Embellish with patterned paper and red cardstock.
5. Computer-generate journal pages and tuck them into the envelopes.

" I wanted to create with 'rescued relatives'.

What is a *Rescued Relative*? Well....

I began collecting vintage photographs about four years ago. I stumbled across my first one in a small basket at the top of the stairs in an antique shop. Since then, I have amassed quite a collection and use them frequently in my artwork.

I call the people in these photos my 'rescued relatives' because I feel I've rescued them from oblivion. It is hard to think that they had been 'discarded' somewhere along the way … these lost souls deserve to be **rescued**. I collect photographs that speak to me … usually this means an interesting facial expression or a familiar face. If I can look at a picture and envision knowing the person, it usually means it's coming home with me. " Amy

Otto Amy Wellenstein
Dimensional Gift Tag

Materials:

Black and White Cardstock: Bazzill

Rust and Slate Adirondack Inkpads: Ranger Industries

Platinum MetalExtra Inkpad: ColorBox by Clearsnap

Onyx Black VersaFine Inkpad: Tsukineko

Decorator Chalks: Craf-T Products

Rubber Stamps: "Otto" by Stampotique Originals; Script #59-365: "Tin Can" Mail by Stampa Rosa; Italian Text by Rubber Baby Buggy Bumpers

Typewriter Key: Paper Bliss by Westrim

Adhesives: The Ultimate! Glue

Other: Mat board, small matchbox drawer and a scrap of black aluminum screen

Instructions:

1. Stamp "Otto" on white cardstock using black ink; color with chalks and trim to fit in matchbox drawer.

2. Cut a frame from cardstock to fit over the top of the matchbox; stamp frame with Italian text using platinum ink.

3. Line frame with black aluminum screen and glue to the top of the matchbox.

4. Cut a small house-shaped tag from mat board; sponge on rust and slate inks.

5. Stamp tag with script using black ink.

6. Glue matchbox to the tag; glue typewriter key above matchbox.

Modern Woman Amy Wellenstein
Dimensional Gift Tag

Materials:

Black and White Cardstock: Bazzill

Lavendar Inkpad: Vivid by Clearsnap

Pink and Platinum MetalExtra Inkpads: ColorBox by Clearsnap

Onyx Black VersaFine Inkpad: Tsukineko

Decorator Chalks: Craf-T Products

Rubber Stamps: "Modern Woman" and "Measuring Tape" by Stampotique Originals; Script #JV142G by Limited Edition Rubber Stamps

Eyelet Alphabet and Charmed Photo Corners (Dots): Making Memories

Adhesive: The Ultimate! Glue

Other: Mat board, small matchbox drawer and a scrap of black aluminum screen

Instructions:

1. Stamp "Modern Woman" on white cardstock using black ink; color with chalks and trim to fit in matchbox drawer.

2. Cut a frame from cardstock to fit over the top of the matchbox. Stamp frame with script using platinum ink.

3. Line frame with black aluminum screen and glue to the top of the matchbox.

4. Cut a small house-shaped tag from mat board; sponge on pink and lavender inks.

5. Stamp "Measuring Tape" along both sides of the tag using black ink.

6. Glue matchbox and photo corner to the tag. Set a small alphabet charm below the photo corner.

These tags started out as Christmas ornaments. But, as is often the case, I got on a roll and made way too many. I was trying to figure out what to do with all the extras and then it hit me ... what wonderful gift tags they'd make. It also meant that the recipient could use them as ornaments on their tree ... and enjoy them for years to come. If you make them for family and friends, consider using photos to personalize them instead of stamped images. Amy

Olive Rose Amy Wellenstein
Dimensional Gift Tag

Materials:

Black and White Cardstock: Bazzill

Banana and Sepia Archival Inkpads: Ranger Industries

Chartreuse Impress Inkpad: Tsukineko

Platinum MetalExtra Inkpad: ColorBox by Clearsnap

Onyx Black VersaFine Inkpad: Tsukineko

Decorator Chalks: Craf-T Products

Rubber Stamps: "Olive Rose," "Alpha," "Antique Border," and "Love Definition" by Stampotique Originals

Silver Brads and Black Eyelet: Making Memories

"Wish" Word Charm: Local Craft Store

Adhesive: The Ultimate! Glue

Other: Mat board, small matchbox drawer and a scrap of black aluminum screen

Instructions:

1. Stamp "Olive Rose" on white cardstock using black ink; color with chalks and trim to fit in matchbox drawer.

2. Cut a frame from cardstock to fit over the top of the matchbox; stamp frame with "Love Definition" using platinum ink.

3. Line frame with black aluminum screen and glue to the top of the matchbox.

4. Cut a small house-shaped tag from mat board; sponge on banana and chartreuse inks.

5. Stamp tag with "Alpha" using black ink and antique border using sepia ink.

6. Set an eyelet at the top of the tag and use brads to attach a word charm; glue matchbox to tag below the word charm.

Panoramic Travel Journal

Amy Wellenstein

Materials:

Journal: 7gypsies

Pale Pink Paper: Rusty Pickle

Black Cardstock: Bazzill

"Dictionary Travel" Strips (Adventure) and "Travel" Bits & Pieces (Destination): Real Life Cardstock Stickers: Pebbles, Inc.

Brads and Eyelets (1/8" and 1/16"): Making Memories

Metal Accents Frame: Marcella by Kay

Adhesives: UHU Glue Stick; Scotch Double-Stick Tape

Other: Photograph, sandpaper, small square of chipboard and waxed linen cord

Instructions:

1. Use glue stick to adhere pink paper to the cover of the journal.

2. Adhere a sticker border (Adventure) across the top of the journal.

3. Adhere a sticker "label holder" (Destination) to the bottom of the cover. Embellish with brads.

4. Use sandpaper to lightly distress a photograph from a past vacation.

5. Reinforce a small square of black cardstock with chipboard. Adhere the photograph to the black cardstock.

6. Use double-stick tape to attach a metal frame over the photo.

7. Set a mini-eyelet on either side of the frame. Tie a piece of waxed linen cord through each eyelet.

8. Set two eyelets on each side of the cover. Run the waxed linen cord through the eyelets and tie to secure.

"The photo on the cover of this journal was taken on Santa Catalina Island. My husband and I often take our boat over from Long Beach to Avalon Harbor. This print was altered slightly with sandpaper and markers to accentuate the blue sky and give it an aged appearance." Amy

Materials:

Journal: 7gypsies

Maps Paper: Sonnets by Sharen Soneff/ Creative Imaginations

Wordz (2001): Danelle Johnson/Creative Imaginations

Journey Defined (Discover): Making Memories

"Travel Labels" (Road Trip) and "Family" Bits & Pieces (Sisters): Real Life Cardstock Stickers by Pebbles, Inc.

Domed Random Alphabet Reversed (Blue Water): Life's Journey by K&Company

Inkjet Transparency: Apollo

Onyx Black VersaFine Inkpad: Tsukineko

"Handprint" Alphabet Stamps: Turtle Press

Brads and Large Square Page Pebble: Making Memories

"On the Road" Metal Message: Li'l Davis Designs

Adhesives: UHU Glue Stick; Scotch Double-Stick Tape

Other: Photos and sandpaper

Instructions:

1. Glue map patterned paper to both pages.

2. Scan a vacation photo and print it on transparency film. Use glue stick to attach the transparency to the bottom of the right page.

3. Layer the "Discover" definition sticker on a strip of sandpaper. Attach the strip to the right page using brads.

4. Stamp the name of the location above the strip using alphabet stamps. Attach dimensional stickers that are relevant to the trip ("Blue Water" and "2001").

5. Use sandpaper to distress two photographs. Attach the photos to the left page using brads. Embellish the photos with alphabet stamps and a metal message ("on the road").

6. Adhere a large square Page Pebble over the front of a third photograph; use double-stick tape to layer this photo on the left page between the others.

7. Embellish the left page with stickers ("sisters" and "ROAD TRIP").

Panoramic Travel Journal
(Pages One and Two)

"The 'Mexico' spread in this journal features vacation photos of my younger sister, Vicki, and I. Each year she visits we try to do something fun and exciting. This particular year, our destination was Puerto Penasco, Mexico. We rode the ATC along the beach all day, barbequed fresh shrimp, and just relaxed ... it was fantastic. I'm taken back to that weekend every time I look at these photos." Amy

Panoramic Travel Journal (Pages Three and Four)

Materials:

Journal: 7gypsies

Days Gone By Paper: Karen Foster Designs

Black Maruyama Paper: Magenta

Dictionary Family: Pebbles Inc.

Brown Cardstock: Bazzill

Window Keeper: Rebecca Sower Nostalgiques "The Attic Collection" by EK Success

Wordz (2003): Danelle Johnson / Creative Imaginations

"Travel" Sampler (A Journey), "Dictionary Travel" Labels (Relaxing), "Travel" Bits & Pieces (Scenic) and "Travel" Labels (Vacation): Real Life Cardstock Stickers by Pebbles, Inc.

"Travels" Metal Message: Li'l Davis Designs

"Destination" Paper Clips: Rebecca Sower Nostaliques "The Attic Collection" by EK Success

Adhesives: UHU Glue Stick; Scotch Double-Stick Tape; Black Masking Tape

Other: Photos and sandpaper

Instructions:

1. Glue script patterned paper to both pages.

2. Use sandpaper to distress three photographs. Layer two photos on brown cardstock and adhere them to the left page.

3. Embellish the photos on the left page with metal messages ("travels"), stickers ("scenic") and a decorative paper clip.

4. Further embellish the page with stickers ("relaxing" and "VACATION").

5. Adhere a sticker border ("A Journey") along the top of the right page.

6. Attach the third photo to the left page using black masking tape.

7. Adhere a swatch of black maruyama paper next to the photo. Adhere a window keeper to the maruyama.

8. Cut patterned paper into a tag shape. Adhere a small photo to the "tag" and insert it into the window keeper.

9. Embellish the window keeper with a dimensional sticker or date.

"The "Hotel Barracuda" spread in this journal shows photos from a 2003 vacation to Cozumel, Mexico. My husband and I were **engaged** *in Cozumel in 2001 and returned to relive the experience. He* **proposed** *in the middle of the San Gervasio Mayan ruins, which are located in the center of the island. We went back to the very spot ... only this time we lucked out and it wasn't pouring rain! I have a feeling we will visit there* **often** *in the years to come."* Amy

Life is a Journey Box

Materials:

Black Script (Sommes) and White Text (Le Monde) Papers: 7gypsies

Small Square Alpha Charms and Pewter Frame: Making Memories

Adhesives: The Ultimate! Glue; Scotch Double-Stick Tape

Other: Small papier mache box and color copy of vintage photo

Instructions:

1. Use double-stick tape to cover box and lid with patterned paper.

2. Adhere color copy of vintage photo to lid.

3. Glue the pewter frame to lid and embellish with small alpha charms.

Red Letters Box

Materials:

Engraved Fruit Brick Red Diamond Printed Paper: K&Company

Arithmetique Paper: 7gypsies

Small White Coin Envelopes: Local Office Supply

"Love Letters" Die Cuts: Elements by Daisy D's

Freedom Tag Stickers: Life's Journey by K&Company

"Twill Tape Thoughts" Strips: Real Life Cardstock Stickers by Pebbles, Inc.

Small Papier Mache Box: Local Craft Store

Sepia Archival Inkpad: Ranger Industries

Walnut Ink: Paper & Ink

Clear Embossing Powder: Ranger Industries

Text (7150L) Rubber Stamp: Stampotique Originals

Small Numbers (7155A) Rubber Stamp: Nick Bantock / Limited Edition Rubber Stamps

Typewriter Keys: Paper Bliss

Buttons Metal Accents: Marcella by Kay

Adhesives: The Ultimate! Glue; UHU Glue Stick; Scotch Double-Stick Tape; Embossable Tape Sheets by Amy's Magic

Other: Red sealing wax and cotton twine

Instructions:

1. Use glue stick to attach coordinating papers to the base and lid of a papier mache box.

2. Adhere twill sticker strips around the lid of the box.

3. Walnut stain two small white coin envelopes. Stamp with text stamp using sepia ink.

4. Clear emboss a small square in the center of the "Letters" die cut.

5. Tie the die cut and envelopes together using cotton twine. Embellish with sealing wax and a small tag sticker. Adhere to the top of the box with glue.

6. Further embellish the lid of the box by gluing on typewriter keys and metal buttons.

Life is a Journey Box — Amy Wellenstein

Green Shabby Chic Amy Wellenstein
Black Leaf Box

Materials:

Small Papier Mache Box: Local Craft Store

Light Timberline Green and Black Acrylic Paint: Delta Ceramcoat

Clear Top Boss Inkpad: Clearsnap

Clear Embossing Powder: Ranger Industries

Foliate Quad Cube Rubber Stamp: Stampendous

Instructions:

1. Paint the papier mache box and lid black.

2. Clear emboss leaf print all over the box and lid.

3. Paint over the embossed surface with two coats of green paint.

4. Once the paint has dried, scrub the surface with a damp washcloth. The paint will rub off where the box was embossed.

Lovely Girl Amy Wellenstein
Brown Box

Materials:

Brown Stripe Paper, Brown Floral Paper and Tea Dye Letters: Renee Plains "Legacy" by Design Originals

Sommes Black Script Paper: 7gypsies

Small Paper Jewelry Box: Local Craft Store

Slide Mount: Design Originals

Buttons: Local Fabric Store

Adhesives: The Ultimate! Glue; Scotch Double-Stick Tape

Other: Photograph

Instructions:

Use glue stick to attach coordinating papers to the base and lid of a paper jewelry box.

Cover a slide mount with tan patterned paper. Adhere the photo to the back of the slide mount. Layer the slide mount on black patterned paper, then adhere it to the lid of the box. Glue buttons in the four corners. Computer-generate "lovely" and attach below the slide mount with glue stick.

Together Amy Wellenstein
Green Box

Materials:

Bella Folk Art Printed Flat Paper: K&Company

Script Die Cut Paper Sheet: Marcella by Kay

"Ribbon Checked" Paper Strips: Real Life Cardstock Stickers by Pebbles, Inc.

"Dictionary Love" Labels: Real Life Cardstock Stickers by Pebbles, Inc.

Small Papier Mache Box: Local Craft Store

Brads: Local Craft Store

Label Holder: Making Memories

Adhesives: Scotch Double-Stick Tape, Glue Stick

Instructions:

1. Use glue stick to attach patterned paper to the base and lid of papier mache box.

2. Adhere brown checked sticker strips around the lid of the box. Attach die cut button border around the lid above the sticker strips.

3. Adhere a sticker word ("together") to the front of the box.

4. Use brads to secure a label holder over the sticker word.

Shabby Chic Amy Wellenstein
White Box

Materials:

Small Papier Mache Box: Local Craft Store

Magnolia White and Black Acrylic Paint: Delta Ceramcoat

Clear Top Boss Inkpad: Clearsnap

Clear Embossing Powder: Ranger Industries

"Fax to Wolfgang" (Large) Rubber Stamp: Stampotique Originals

Instructions:

1. Paint the papier mache box and lid black.

2. Clear emboss text all over the box and lid.

3. Paint over the embossed surface with two coats of magnolia white paint.

4. Once the paint has dried, scrub the surface with a damp washcloth. The paint will rub off where the box was embossed.

"I love giving gifts in special packaging ... these embellished boxes are some wonderful examples. The recipient is really getting two gifts in one, since they can re-use the 'wrapping.' Whenever possible, I like to incorporate photographs ... this makes for a much more personal gift. Amy

Helga Strauss resides is beautiful Victoria, BC, Canada, with her wonderful fiancée, James, and darling cat, Pablo. She owns and operates an online shop called ARTchix Studio that specializes in vintage images and artsy embellishments for the mixed media artist. She also co-publishes a fun magazine called *ARTitude Zine* that focuses on honoring the creative side in all of us. She holds a BA degree in Art History from the University of Oregon. She works in all kinds of art media: oils, acrylics, paper, found objects and pretty much anything she can get her hands on.

Helga writes: "My Mom introduced me to the rubber stamp world about five years ago. It wasn't long before I started participating in and hosting art swaps. What a fun addiction! I shared tons of artwork with wonderful artists from around the world. I slowly started integrating some of the vintage images from my vast postcard collection into my artwork. I struck on the idea that perhaps I could sell collage sheets after fellow swap artists kept asking me where they could get images like mine. Alas, ARTchix Studio was born! I started out with just four collage sheets. And now I have over 500 items for sale on my website. In addition, a few years ago, my swap buddy, Suz Simanaitis, and I joined forces to publish ARTitude Zine, a magazine devoted to highlighting mixed arts like altered books, collage, assemblage, artist trading cards, scrapbooking and rubber stamping. I wake up with a smile every day because I absolutely love what I do."

My fiancée and I went to Guatemala for a very special vacation together. While there, we took the gorgeous photo of the door you see on this journal. We later turned it into a transparency image for our business, ARTchix Studio. Helga

Materials:

Journal: 7gypsies

Vintage Ledger Page and Mini Mix Collage Sheet: ARTchix Studio

Thin Cardboard: Local Craft Store

"Latin America" Transparency: ARTchix Studio

Coal Dye Inkpad: Ancient Page by Clearsnap

Watercolor Crayons: Caran d'Ache

Alphabet Rubber Stamps: PSX

Hand-Dyed Ribbon: "Red Hot" by ARTchix Studio

Pewter Key and Pewter Spiral Frame Charm: ARTchix Studio

Adhesives: Xyron 900 with Permanent Adhesive Cartridge; Neutral pH Adhesive by Lineco Inc.; Judi Kins Diamond Glaze

Tools: Awl, watercolor brush and pliers

Instructions:

Score and tear vintage ledger pages to roughly the size of the journal, using the journal cover as a guide. Adhere to the journal with Neutral pH Adhesive. Cut out transparency image of door, then cut it in half and run it through a Xyron machine to apply a permanent adhesive to the back. Press onto the journal cover into place. Scribble brown watercolor crayons around the edges of the cover, then blend with a bit of water and a watercolor brush. With an awl, make two holes in the center edges of the journal. Thread hand-dyed ribbon through the holes and tie into a bow. Slide a key charm onto one end of the ribbon and make a knot to hold it in place. Before tying the photo charm onto the other end of the ribbon, bend back its backside prongs with pliers and insert a little image cut to size. It's best if the image is first adhered to a thin piece of cardboard. Bend backside prongs back down and apply a few drops of Diamond Glaze over the front of the image; let dry and tie it onto the other end of the ribbon.

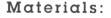

Journal
My Journey
Helga Strauss

For Aunt Sally Helga Strauss
Tag

Materials:

Tag: Local Office Supply

"My Sweet Angel" Transparency:
ARTchix Studio

Lime Green Silk Ribbon: Treenway Silks

"Made For You" Copper Tag:
ARTchix Studio

Adhesive: UHU Glue Stick

Other: Vintage copper tinsel garland

Tools: Scissors and hole punch

Instructions:

Lay the "My Sweet Angel" transparency image onto a plain shipping tag. Cut the transparency image to the same size as the shipping tag, using the tag as a guide. Punch a hole at the top through the transparency. Thread a length of vintage tinsel garland through the transparency and shipping tag and tie at the top. Glue computer-generated words onto the front of the transparency. Punch two small holes in the lower right corner through the transparency and shipping tag. Thread a length of silk ribbon through the holes and tie on the copper tag.

" I love making gift tags! You can wrap your gifts in inexpensive, plain brown wrap or colored bags, add a colorful handmade tag and watch it come to life! Impress your friends and family with this unique gift wrap style. Plus the tags look great hanging on fridges and memo boards, etc., so they're really a gift that keeps on giving. " Helga

My Love Helga Strauss
Card

Materials:

Heart Card: ARTchix Studio

"Hold Me" Transparency: ARTchix Studio

Watercolor Crayons: Caran d'Ache

Embroidery Floss: DMC

Adhesives: UHU Glue Stick; Terrifically Tacky Tape

Other: Seed beads

Tools: Embroidery needle, awl, utility knife, ruler, cutting matt and watercolor brush

Instructions:

Cut a rectangle window into the heart card using a utility knife, ruler and cutting matt to protect your work surface. Cut two small strips of Terrifically Tacky Tape. Adhere tape to the top and bottom of the transparency image and affix to the heart card. With an awl, make holes around the window frame. Then use needle and embroidery floss to sew seed beads around the window frame of the card. Computer-generate "my love" and adhere with a UHU Glue Stick. Scribble watercolor crayons around the edge of the card and blend with a bit of water and a watercolor brush.

True Friendships Tag

Helga Strauss

The little girl in this tag tends to pop up in a lot of my artwork. Her photo was taken in the early 1900s and I have no idea who she is, but I just adore her. I thought this tag would be perfect for giving to a special friend. The ribbon at the top makes it easy to hang on a lamp, cabinet knob, etc.

Helga

Materials:

"Faces From the Past" Collage Sheet: ARTchix Studio

Tag: Local Craft Store

Crimson Velvet Leaves: ARTchix Studio

Hand-Dyed Ribbon: "Red Hot" by ARTchix Studio

Embroidery Floss: DMC

Adhesive: Aleene's Tacky Glue

Other: Fabrics, vintage buttons and fortune from Chinese fortune cookie

Tools: Needle and hole punch

Instructions:

Rip green fabric to shape of the tag, using the tag as a guide. Adhere green fabric to tag with Tacky Glue. Add an additional torn piece of fabric at the bottom with Tacky Glue. Glue velvet leaves (used as wings) to the tag. Cut out and glue down little girl image into place. Glue down paper fortune. Use needle and embroidery floss to sew on buttons. Punch holes at the top of the tag. Thread a length of hand-dyed ribbon through the holes for easy hanging.

I designed a card almost exactly like this for my wedding invitations. The only difference was that I stamped 'celebrate our hearts' instead of 'I adore you.' And I used a transparency image that included a beautiful bride and groom. This card can be modified for any special event or holiday. Just place a transparency image of your choice in the window card, frame it with glittery dots, add ribbon and stamp a favorite phrase. So easy and fun! Helga

I Adore You Card
Helga Strauss

Materials:

Window Card: ARTchix Studio

"Hold Me" Transparency: ARTchix Studio

Coal Dye Inkpad: Ancient Page by Clearsnap

Original Art Glittering System in Ultra Fine 169: Urchin by The Art Institute

Antique Alphabet Rubber Stamp Set: PSX

Hand-Dyed Ribbon: "Caribbean Ocean" by ARTchix Studio

Adhesives: The Art Glittering System Adhesive by The Art Institute; Terrifically Tacky Tape

Tools: Utility knife and ruler

Instructions:

Cut out "Hold Me" transparency image. Cut two tiny squares of Terrifically Tacky Tape. Adhere tape to the top and bottom of the transparency and affix to inside of card. Make little dots of glue around window frame. Sprinkle ultra fine glitter onto dots; let dry. Stamp the words "I Adore You" using Ancient Page inkpad. Cut two slits in the central back of the card using utility knife and ruler, then thread hand-dyed ribbon throough the slits and tie in a bow.

Product Resource Guide

100 Proof Press: www.100proofpress.com

3 Sisters / Moda Fabrics: www.modafabrics.com

3M / Scotch: www.scotchbrand.com

7gypsies: www.sevengypsies.com

A Lost Art: Local Craft Store

A Stamp in the Hand Co.: www.astampinthehand.com

Aleene's Tacky Glue / Duncan Crafts: www.duncancrafts.com

All Night Media/Plaid: www.allnightmedia.com

American Tag: www.americantag.net

American Traditional Stencils: www.americantraditional.com

Amy's Magic: Local Craft Store

Angy's Dreams: www.angysdreams.it

Anima Designs: www.animadesigns.com

Anna Griffin: www.annagriffin.com

Antiquities Ink: www.rangerink.com

Art Impressions: www.artimpressions.com

Art Institute, The: Local Craft Store

Art Warehouse: Local Craft Store

ARTchix Studio: www.artchixstudio.com

Artsy Collage Gel: Local Craft Store

Avery Dennison Corporation: www.avery.com

Barnes & Noble: www.barnesandnoble.com

Bazzill Basics Paper: www.bazzillbasics.com

Black Ink: www.dickblick.com

Carl Mfg Co. Ltd: www.carl-officeproducts.com

Canson: www.canson.com

Chatterbox, Inc.: www.chatterboxinc.com

Claudia Rose: Local Craft Store

Clearsnap, Inc.: www.clearsnap.com

Color Textiles: www.colortextiles.com

Colorbok: www.colorbok.com

Colors by Design: www.colorsbydesign.com

Coptic Markers: Local Craft Store or Office Supply

Craf-T Products: www.craf-tproducts.com

Crafter's Pick: www.crafterspick.com

Crafters Edition: Local Craft Store

Creative Imaginations: www.cigift.com

Creative Impressions: www.creativeimpressions.com

Creative Tags: Local Craft Store

Daisy D's Paper Co: www.daisydspaper.com

Darice: www.darice.com

Delta: www.deltacrafts.com

Design Originals: www.d-originals.com

Dizzy Frizzy: Local Craft Store

DMC: www.dmc-usa.com

DMD Industries: www.dmdind.com

Dymo: www.dymo.com

E-6000 Craft Adhesive/Eclectic Products: 1-800-767-4667

EK Success: www.eksuccess.com

Ever After Scrapbook Company: www.addictedtoscrapbooking.com until www.everafterscrapbook.com is available

Fancifuls, Inc.: www.fancifulsinc.com

Far and Away: www.farandawayscrapbooks.com

Fiskars: www.fiskars.com

FoofaLa: www.foofala.com 1-800-588-6707

Forget Me Knot: 254-773-3337

Fresco: Local Craft Store

GE Silicone Household Glue: Local Craft or Hardware Store

Gem Tac Permanent Adhesive / Beacon: www.beaconcreates.com

Glue Dots International LLC: www.gluedots.com

Golden Artist Colors: www.goldenpaints.com

Hermafix: 1-888-CENTIS-6

Hero Arts: www.heroarts.com

Hyko Products: Local Craft Store

Impress Rubber Stamps: www.impressrubberstamps.com

Jacquard Products: www.jacquardproducts.com

Jewel Craft: Local Craft Store

JHB International: www.buttons.com

JKM Ribbons and Trims: www.jkmribbon.com

Jolee's by You Sticko Stickers: www.eksuccess.com

Judi Kins: www.judikins.com

K&Company: www.kandcompany.com

Karen Foster Design: www.karenfosterdesign.com

KI Memories: www.kimemories.com

Li'l Davis Designs: www.lildavisdesigns.com

Limited Edition Rubber Stamps: www.limitededitionrubberstamps.com

Lineco, Inc: www.lineco.com

Liquitex: www.liquitex.com

Loew Cornell, Inc.: www.loew-cornell.com

GROW 1. to come into being or be produced naturally 2. to develop to thrive, as a living thing 3. to increase in size, quantity

GARDEN

ALWAYS IN MY HEART

memories

Product Resource Guide Continued

Lost Aussie Designs: www.lostaussie.com

Magenta: www.magentarubberstamps.com

Magic Scraps: www.magicscraps.com

Making Memories: www.makingmemories.com

Marcella by Kay: Local Craft Store

Marvy Uchida: www.uchida.com

MaVinci's Reliquary: www.crafts.dm.net/mall/reliquary

Millikan: Local Craft Store

Mod Podge by Plaid:
www.allnighmedia.com

Morex Corporation: Local Craft Store

Mundial: Local Craft Store

Mustard Moon: www.mustardmoon.com

My Mind's Eye: www.frame-ups.com

Nick Bantock: www.rangerink.com

Offray: www.offray.com

Our Lady of Rubber: 520-432-2229

P&B Textiles: www.pbtex.com

Paper Bliss by Westrim: www.westrimcrafts.com

Paper Company, The: www.thepaperco.com

Paper Cuts: www.papercutsthescrapbookstore.com

Paper Fever: www.paperfever.com

Paper Inspirations: Local Craft Store

Paper Loft: www.paperloft.com

Paper Passions: www.paperpassions.net

Paperbag Studios: www.paperbagstudios.com

Pebbles Inc.: www.pebblesinc.com

Pellon Consumer Products: www.pellonideas.com

Penny Black Rubber Stamps: www.pennyblackinc.com

Pioneer: www.pioneerphotoalbums.com

Plaid Enterprises, Inc.: www.plaidonline.com

Postmodern Designs: 405-321-3176

Printworks: www.printworkscollection.com

ProArt: Local Craft or Camera Store

Provo Craft: www.provocraft.com

Prym-Dritz Corporation: www.dritz.com

PSX: www.psxdesign.com

Quickutz: www.quickutz.com

Ranger Industries, Inc.: www.rangerink.com

River City Rubberworks: Local Craft Store

Rocky Mountain Scrapbook Co: Local Craft Store

Rubber Baby Buggy Bumpers: www.rubberbaby.com

Rubber Stampede: www.rubberstampede.com

Rubber Stamps of America: www.stampusa.com

Rubbermoon Stamp Company: www.rubbermoon.com

Rusty Pickle: www.rustypickle.com

Sakura: www.sakuraofamerica.com

Sanford Sharpies: Local Craft Store or Office Supply

Scrap Ease: 1-800-274-3874

SEI, Inc.: www.shopsei.com

Sobo Craft & Fabric Glue: Local Craft Store

Somerset Studios: www.stampington.com

Stampa Barbara: Local Craft Store

Stampa Rosa: www.creativebeginnings.com

Stampers Anonymous:
www.stampersanonymous.com

Stampington & Company: www.stampington.com

Stampotique Originals: www.stampotique.com

Stewart Superior Corporation:
www.stewartsuperior.com

Strathmore Artist Papers:
www.strathmoreartist.com

Terrifically Tacky Tape: Local Craft Store

Treasure Cay: home.tampabay.rr.com/tcayarts

Tsukineko: www.tsukineko.com

USArtQuest, Inc.: www.usartquest.com

Vintage Charmings: www.vintagecharmings.com

Wimpole Street Creations: www.barrett-house.com

Wordsworth: www.wordsworthstamps.com

Xyron: www.xyron.com

Yes! Paste / Gane Brothers: www.ganebrothers.com